CHARLES DICKERSON

The

Aldrich Saga

Order this book online at www.trafford.com
or email orders@trafford.com

Most Trafford titles are also available at major online book retailers.

Print information available on the last page.

ISBN: 978-1-4120-3526-2 (sc)
ISBN: 978-1-4122-2683-7 (e)

Trafford rev. 01/25/2023

 www.trafford.com
North America & international
toll-free: 844-688-6899 (USA & Canada)
fax: 812 355 4082

I dedicate this book to my wife, Joan Dickerson,
who was a marvelous editor and advisor.

Introduction

To anyone who might give a tinker's damn, my name is Charles Dickerson, and I'm the guy who wrote this book. I was born in the village of Vista, Missouri, in 1921. My father was a telegrapher on the Frisco Railroad. My mother, Audrey, died in 1930 of spinal meningitis, leaving me and my brother, Nelson. After Dad lost his job on the Frisco Railroad because of seniority, he and I moved, in 1931, to live with Dad's mother, Sara Dickerson, in Aldrich, Missouri. Nelson remained with Audrey's mother in Kansas City.

I started school in Aldrich in the fourth grade, dressed in knickers and golf socks. Several students made fun of my attire, while other students wanted to fight me. They gave me a now moniker. I was called "the Kansas City kid." Very soon I learned that large city schools were far different from country schools like Aldrich. I implored Dad to buy me some Big Smith overalls like the other boys wore, but all my entreaties fell on deaf ears, even though the overalls I wanted cost less than $1 a pair.

Dad, I know ,was embarrassed by his lack of funds, and I felt sorry for him. Eventually, though, I became the proud owner of two pair of Big Smith overalls, made possible by Dad's new income from bootlegging. It wasn't all peaches and cream, however, because some of the students would, from time to time, yell, "You're dad's a bootlegger." I mostly ignored them.

My home with Grandma Dickerson continued for seven years, until 1939, when I graduated from high school. In 1938, Dad had been able to renew his telegrapher's job, for by now the Depression was starting to moderate.

Dad now had a new wife, Hamey O'Neil, who would increase our family eventually by three sons and one daughter. When Dad died at 96 years of age, he had made provisions in his will for five sons and one daughter.

I had several mediocre jobs after high school. In 1942, I entered the Navy as an aviation cadet. One year later, I was court-martialed for disciplinary reasons, etc.

I went into the Army Air Force in 1943 and flew thirty-five combat missions as an aerial photographer in the Fifteenth Air Force in Italy. I had the same job Clark Gable had, except I was a tech sergeant, and Gable was a major. My discharge from the Air Force in 1945 was granted on combat points.

The desire I had for attending college came to fruition in August 1946 when I enrolled in the Kansas City, Kansas, junior college. It was here that I met Joan McAmis, a Scotch Irish lass, and married her that same year. To this union, two children were born: Greg, the eldest son, who is now a corporation executive, and Mark, slightly retarded, was a grocery sacker for the Dillon food chain. Mark, three years younger than Greg, was killed in an auto accident in Manhattan, Kansas, in 1983 when he was 32 years old.

Finishing college in 1952 at Kansas State University, my teaching career began in the small high school in Beeler, Kansas, in the fall of 1952. After four years in Beeler, Joan and I received contracts to teach in Sitka, Alaska, which was the original capital of Alaska when the Russians owned Alaska. My job consisted of classroom teaching and being the assistant basketball coach. Sitka would be our home for another four years. Joan and I purchased an old converted ship-to-shore boat used by the Navy to transport Naval officers between ship and shore. We had the boat made into a troller, which we used to ply the inland water ways in our quest for king salmon and halibut.

After two years, I succeeded Bill Marsh as the head basketball coach when he decided to start a doctor's program. I transported the team in twin-engine Grumman airplanes all over southeast Alaska. Because of our retarded son, Mark, and the lack of special education programs in Alaska, Joan and I returned to Manhattan, Kansas, in 1960. I taught in Junction City one year while Joan finished her college work. At the insistence of my insurance agent, I went to Chicago for training and became an All State Insurance agent in Manhattan for two years. At this time, I resumed my teaching career. Joan and I both finished our teaching in Manhattan. We are now retired and living in the Stockton, Missouri, Lake area. I am 82 years old, and Joan is 77.

There are some stories about me, my grandmother, and my father, describing how we lived through the worst depression in the history of our country. Father was unemployed during this era, but Grandmother had an income from Social Security (after it became law in the '30s) of $18 per month. But I did not fail to notice that many of the 250-odd people living in the village displayed more of a benign attitude than one could reasonably expect from people who were locked in such dire circumstances. Most people seemed to laugh and joke at their grievous conditions, and life went on.

I acquired lifelong friendships with many of the people mentioned in these writings, some that I will carry to my grave. I can remember Abe Lincoln's answer when someone asked him about his life. Lincoln replied, "My life is about the short and simple annals of the poor."

While walking through the Pleasant Ridge Cemetery west of Aldrich, where my father and mother are buried, along with my brother and many friends, I thought of the English poem "Ellegy Written in a Country Churchyard" by Thomas Gray. I remembered well one of his epitaphs as he strolled through an English cemetery, witnessing the many graves of the unknown dead.

> *Here rests his head upon the lap of earth.*
> *A youth to fame and fortune unknown.*
> *Fair science frowned not on his humble birth,*
> *And melancholy marked him for her own.*

This could be my epitaph!

Now about the tales you will find in this book. I have used innumerable sources for what you will read. I visited for many years with John Mitchell, who fought all through the Civil War. And then there was my father, who I knew very intimately during the seven years we lived with his mother. We had hundreds of conversations concerning books that we had read, politics, law and stories galore. You should find interest in the true story of Spud Griffin and his revenge on three border ruffians who had mistreated his mother and tried to hang him. The loafers in Aldrich also imparted some interesting tales. My Great Uncle Ira O'Neill told me interesting stories that concerned difficulties suffered by the Irish in early-day America. Clyde Perkins and many other acquaintances made contributions to this book. Almost all of the contributors are dead, but I thank them posthumously anyway.

Then there was Sara O'Neil Dickerson, my grandmother who raised me after my mother died. Sara was born in 1864, the last year of the Civil War. Granny was 12 years old when Custer fought at the Battle of the Little Bighorn, and she remembered when Geronimo began his incursions against the Whites in the 1880s, threatening to kill ten men for every member of his family who had been killed by the Whites.

Granny was 50 years of age when World War I started, sending three of her four sons to combat. My father Ralph was too young, being only 13 years of age in 1914.

Granny remembers when Panchovilla invaded the U.S. village of Columbus, New Mexico, and proceeded to kill eight Americans in 1916. Granny's eldest son was working as a telegrapher in the Southern Pacific Depot when Pancho and his army of 400 men rode into town. Willard told his mother that when he heard shooting and saw a large group of Mexican soldiers on horseback riding around the town. He closed the door of the depot, turned out the light, and remained inside until Pancho and his army left town.

Granny also told me the very interesting story of

Part One

Oh for boyhood's painless play
Sleep that wakes in laughing day,
Health that mocks the doctor's rules
Knowledge never learned of schools.
—John Greenleaf Whittier

Dad and I caught the train for Aldrich on March 13, 1932. We were going there to live with Dad's mother who lived in a small cottage on the side of the big hill above Aldrich. We would stay with Sara, my Dad had explained, until he could get his job back as a telegrapher. Then, we would move, he had promised with a hug.

My Mother had died in Kansas City of spinal meningitis two years earlier, while Dad was gainfully employed by the Frisco Railroad. Since Mother's death, my brother, Nelson, age seven, had resided with Granny Birt, while Dad and I lived in a boarding house in Harrisonville, Missouri. When Dad was bumped from his job in Harrisonville, Granny Dickerson called Dad and told him to come and live with her.

As we waited for the train's departure, Dad reminded me that I had ridden this very train earlier, almost two years to the day, to my Mother's funeral in Aldrich at

Pleasant Ridge. Dad explained that we couldn't have Mother's funeral in a church because spinal meningitis was so contagious. "And, even with a sealed casket, the people who filed by to look at your Mother held handkerchiefs over their mouths."

"Do you remember your Mother's funeral, Charlie?" Dad asked in a whisper.

"Yes, Dad, I remember. I remember how beautiful she looked."

I thought I saw tears in Dad's eyes. It seemed that Dad cried a lot anymore. My reverie was broken. I glanced at my father as the train whistle announced our departure. I thought he looked rather sad, but he turned to me and smiled.

"Charlie, I think you will like living in Aldrich. I grew up there. It's a lot better place to live than Kansas City, and besides, it's the only place we have to go at present. Thank God for Mother."

As I listened to Dad, I began to feel a certain sense of adventure leaving the city. I wondered what a country school would be like. I knew that I would soon find out. As the train meandered through snowy woods, I began to recall some of the things Dad had told me about Aldrich. There was good fishing in Sac River, Dad had said, and there were only 250 people in the town including dogs and cats. Dad had laughingly continued by advising me that the only toilets in Aldrich are outhouses.

"...and, Charlie, you will take your baths in a wash tub with water that you had hand-pumped from the well. You will walk everywhere you go in Aldrich. You will walk to school like Abe Lincoln did, except you won't have to walk as far as he did."

"How far is the school house from Grandmother's?"

"It's probably a quarter of a mile, perhaps a little more."

My thoughts turned to my brother, Nelson, whom I had just parted with at the Kansas City Union Station. I had cried, and so had Granny Birt and Dad. Nelse was only 7 years old and didn't seem to understand that our parting was to be fairly permanent, except for an occasional visit in the summer.

Before we left for the train station that morning, I overheard Granny Birt and Dad discussing Nelse and me living in separate households, and splitting us up, but, as I think back, I can see there was no other way.

Pretty soon, Dad and I struck up another conversation, after Dad finished talking with Charlie Morrison, the conductor. I began to ply Dad with questions.

"Dad, will I be in the fourth grade in Aldrich?"

"Yes."

"Will you take me fishing and hunting?"

"Yes, Charles, we can do a great many things that we couldn't do in the city. If you are poor, as we are, you are better off in a small village in the country. Here, you can go fishing or you can go camping. You can hike across the country. You and I will be able to hunt arrowheads in the Sac River Bottom, for example."

"Will Sara make me eat spinach?"

Dad laughed. "No, honey, but you should learn to eat spinach. It's good for you. Your Grandmother is a great cook. Everything you eat in her house will be good and good for you."

With this last bit of questioning, I fell asleep. It just seemed like a couple of minutes until Dad was shaking me gently, "Charlie, we are here."

I looked around sleepily and saw through the train windows a few lights visible in the gathering dusk. I shall never forget our arrival in Aldrich on that cold March evening. It was snowing heavily. Our walk up the big hill to Sara's house was beautiful. No one seemed to be stirring, and the only sound in the still night was the crunching of the snow beneath our feet.

Grandmother greeted us at the kitchen door and gave me a hug. She looked at Dad and asked how he was.

"Mother, we are fine. How about you? How have you been?"

Sara laughed and said, "Ralph, I'm fine except for the rheumatism."

Dad, with a merry twinkle in his eye, asked Sara if she thought age had anything to do with it.

Sara laughed, looked at me and asked if I was hungry. I said, "Yes, Grandma. The only thing I had to eat on the train was an apple."

Sara remarked that an apple wasn't enough for a growing boy and exclaimed on the depth of the snow.

"It if doesn't stop snowing soon, we won't be able to walk down the hill. My overshoes are worn out."

"Do you have any overshoes, Charles?"

"No, Grandma, and Dad doesn't, either."

Sara laughed again, pleasantly. While Sara set the table, she and Dad carried on a lively conversation. I was pretty much left out of the conversation except Dad did tell me briefly about sliding down the big hill when he was a boy.

"You can really get up a head of steam, Charlie, by the time you get to the bottom of the hill."

"Charles, your dad and his brothers done a lot of sliding down the hill," and she laughed.

"Ralph will have to get some boards and make you a sled."

"Mother, do you still have the featherbed?"

"Yes, Ralph."

"Mother, I haven't slept in a featherbed since I left home."

I looked around Sara's kitchen while she and Dad conversed. There was an aroma of fresh-baked bread in the air, and the warmth of the kitchen was furnished by a glowing cook stove whose top contained a hissing teakettle and a large pot of coffee that was beginning to perk. What a pleasant place, I thought.

And then I remembered that I would enter a new school tomorrow. As Granny served supper, I was wondering what it would be like.

My last thought before I went to sleep in Granny's feather bed was, "Tomorrow I go to a new school."

Needless to say, I did not look forward to my first day of school in Aldrich. I approached the building in a state of quiet alarm. Everyone seemed to be looking at me. I had just come from a big grade school in Kansas City that had about 600 students, where no one had paid any attention to me. Here, everyone seemed to be staring at me. Before the first day was over, I had been given the monicker "The Kansas City Kid." Perhaps it was because I was wearing knickers and golf socks. All the boys seemed to be wearing overalls. I admit that I looked different and was really glad to get my first day of school over with.

When I got home from school, my father greeted me

at the kitchen door inquiring as to how school had gone.

When I told my father what had happened, he grimaced much like he did when I asked him if I was going to get a bicycle. After a couple of hugs, Dad informed me that he would get me some overalls as soon as he could find the money for them.

Granny looked at me and smiled and handed me a fresh-baked cookie.

I was full of despair when I started to school the next morning, feeling that it would be an eternity before I got some overalls. But much to my surprise, several students displayed evidence of friendship that seemed to be sincere. Even students in the upper grades showed some cordiality.

My feeling of well-being was short-lived. When school was out at 3 o'clock, as I stepped off of the school grounds, I was immediately challenged to my first fight. The kid who made the challenge was as scared of me as I was of him. I knew that when I socked him and he began to cry. For this altercation, both my adversary and I received a spanking from the fifth-grade teacher.

When I got home, Dad, as usual, greeted me and wanted to know how things went at school. I wondered if Dad had heard of the fight and my spanking, as I speculated on an answer to his question.

"Fine, Dad. People were more friendly." I searched his face and was satisfied he hadn't heard about the day's events.

Dad did tell me at the supper table to quit eating so fast and continued his conversation by telling me he had finished a book by Victor Hugo about the French Revolution. I think you would be interested in the story," he had remarked.

Things at school began to loosen up a little bit, and then I met Marion Mitchell, one of my fifth-grade classmates. I can't remember the catalyst for our meeting, but soon we were walking home together, the best of buddies. While conversing, we discovered we had several things in common. We both liked airplanes, camping and fishing. Besides that, Marion informed me that his Grandfather Mitchell had fought in the Civil War and he had the pistol he had used during the war.

My knowledge of the Civil War was rather scant, but I was very interested in seeing a man who had fought in that war. And to think, he had the gun that he had used in fighting the war. Marion informed me that when I came to his house he would take me to see his grandfather and show me his grandfather's gun.

School would soon be over for the summer, I thought, and Marion and I discussed our summer plans.

The first time Mitch took me to see Uncle John Mitchell, as he was affectionately known in the Village of Aldrich, he was sitting on his front porch in a straight-back hickory chair. He was wearing a black coat, black trousers and a black hat. His not-so-white shirt was open at the collar. I wondered why he didn't wear a tie with his suit. In Kansas City, where I had been living, people wore ties with their suits. He seemed to be sorta dressed up, other than the lack of a tie. He was thin like a rapier blade. I turned my attention to his face. He really looked old, I thought. He sat very straight in his chair with his cane thrust out in front of him, as if he wanted to be able to flee at a moment's notice.

"Grandpa, this is Charles Dickerson," Marion said quickly. And then, as an afterthought, Marion moved closer to his grandfather, speaking directly into Uncle John's good ear.

"Charles has come to Aldrich to live with his grandmother, Sara Dickerson. He's my age," Marion continued confidently. "We are in the same grade in school."

Uncle John tapped his cane lightly, and without looking at me, wanted to know my age.

Marion answered his grandfather, almost shouting, "He is the same age I am, Grandpa. He's 11 years old."

Marion smiled at me. "Grandpa doesn't always hear me. His hearing isn't very good."

John Mitchell was staring at me with his faded blue eyes. His skin was so white and sickly looking, as Granny would say, and I wondered why he didn't wear glasses.

After an interminable time, Uncle John looked away from me.

"I know Sara Dickerson," he said softly.

"Where did you fight in the Civil War, Uncle John?" I asked hesitantly. He ignored my question.

"Sara was a young woman when I came to Aldrich," he said slowly, as if he remembered more than his comment. "A real pretty woman. I remember her." He said again, "a real pretty woman."

Mitch grinned and explained that Grandpa probably didn't hear my question.

"To answer your question," Mitch continued, "I know that Grandfather fought in the battle of Nashville, Tenn., but I'm not sure of what other battles he fought in."

Bolstered by my apparent interest, Mitch began to relate other bits of interest concerning his grandfather's participation in the Civil War.

"Uncle John was born in Arkansas. I'm not sure where in Arkansas. Grandpa doesn't seem to remember. He joined the Union Army when he was 14 years old in Burlington, Iowa, enlisting in the 9th Iowa Cavalry."

"Wow! How do you know all that?" I asked.

"Grandpa tells me every so often the things that I'm telling you. I reckon that he doesn't want to forget."

Mitch continued the conversation by telling me that Uncle John was 29 years old when the Battle of the Little Bighorn was fought. "You know, Dick, that's the battle where the Indians killed General Custer."

By now, Mitch really had my attention.

"Mitch, you called me Dick. You've never called me that before."

"Your last name is Dickerson; I just shortened your last name."

"OK, Mitch. I'll call you Mitch, and you can call me Dick."

Mitch grinned and continued by stating Uncle John was 43 years old when the Battle of Wounded Knee was fought up in South Dakota, the last Indian battle with the Army.

"You mean, Mitch, he was only 14 years old when he joined the Army?" I asked in astonishment.

"Yes."

Over the course of the morning, Mitch told me several things about his grandfather. "Uncle John draws a pension of $100 a month for fighting in the war," Mitch explained, "but some of the Civil War veterans around here don't get any pension at all."

"Mitch, why don't they get a pension, too?"

"Because they fought for the South. It has something

to do with the 14th Amendment in the Constitution. Grandpa wants to live long enough to be the last living Civil War veteran."

"Do you think he can live that long, Mitch?"

"I don't know. He's older than any other Civil War veteran I know of that lives around here."

As I visited with Mitch, I would occasionally glance at Uncle John. He sat immobile, staring straight ahead, as if we weren't there. He had made no effort to take part in the conversation.

"Mitch, you said your grandpa was 86 years old and he was born in 1847."

"That's what it says on his gravestone."

"Does he have a gravestone already?"

"Yes."

"He isn't dead yet."

"When he dies, the gravestone will be there."

Other questions came to mind that I would have liked to ask Mitch, but our conversation ended with Marion asking his grandpa for a quarter.

"I'll get your tobacco today, Grandpa."

Uncle John produced a quarter from an assemblage of loose coins in his pocket.

"Get Old Advertiser," Uncle John enjoined, without looking at Mitch or me.

"I will," Marion replied, as he motioned me to follow him. As we left his porch, I glanced back at Uncle John. He did not seem to be aware of our departure.

As we made our way toward Toalson's Grocery Store, Mitch explained that we could buy six sacks of Old Advertiser for a quarter. "We'll give Grandpa five sacks, and we will keep one sack to smoke. Grandpa doesn't know about the extra sack of Old Advertiser." Mitch grinned, "Do you know how to roll a cigarette?"

"No," I replied earnestly. "Do you?"

"Sure, I know how. I'll roll one for you."

"I've never smoked, Mitch," I said rather softly. "Smoking isn't good for you, is it?"

Mitch answered me rather matter-of-factly, "All of the men around Aldrich smoke. It doesn't seem to hurt them."

After delivering Uncle John's tobacco, which the old veteran took without comment, Mitch took me up the street to his workshop, or shed, as he sometimes called it, to partake of an Old Advertiser cigarette. As promised, Mitch rolled me a cigarette and proceeded to light if for me. I watched Mitch as he lit his cigarette and took a few puffs. I tried to emulate his actions, but I got smoke in my nose and began to cough. Mitch gave me some quick directions on holding the cigarette and the best method for taking a puff.

"You need to inhale lightly until you get used to it. Don't inhale too deeply at first." As I listened to Mitch's instruction, I felt that I would learn to smoke quickly.

Mitch walked over to the shed door, which was closed, and peeped through a knot hole in the door."

"What are you looking at, Mitch?"

"I'm checking out the landscape." Mitch looked serious. "I don't want my mother to come out and catch us smoking."

I had noticed the back door of the Mitchell kitchen was only a few yards from the shed door, so it was in Mitch's shed that I first learned to smoke, and unknowingly, Uncle Sam was paying for the tobacco, via Uncle John.

As the summer days stretched toward autumn, my

friendship with Mitch grew. In just a few weeks' time, we had plans for building a boat to be used for trapping muskrat on the river, and we had anticipated when we could raise the money for the purchase of a dozen new No. 1 steel traps from the Montgomery Ward catalog.

A letter from Granny Birt solved our money problem by sending me a check for $5. The only stipulation was a promise from me to sing in the school glee club.

Mitch's remark, upon hearing of my good fortune, was, "Now we can trap the river when we finish the boat."

Life was indeed, as my father had promised, much more exciting than my life in Kansas City had been.

One Saturday morning Granny said I could walk down the big hill to town with her. I think she understood that I was rather skittish about going downtown because Carl Hensley had issued a challenge to me to come and fight him in the Christian Church yard. Thus far, I had failed to accept his challenge. When Granny and I reached the middle of town, there was Carl with a couple of other kids. As Carl approached me, I could see that he was engaged in eating a rather large triple decker ice cream cone.

"What about the fight?" Carl asked.

"Get out of here," Granny Dickerson motion to Carl with her parasol. "You leave Charles alone."

Bill Hensley, the big brother of Carl, rode by on his bicycle and remarked that I was hiding behind my grandmother's skirt.

Again, Carl repeated his challenge, "When are you

gonna fight me?"

I looked at Carl's smiling face and his large ice cream cone. I swung quickly, knocking Carl off his balance, and his ice cream cone went flying.

Bill rode up close to Sara and screamed, "Let 'em fight."

Granny swung her parasol toward Bill and told him to "get out of here!" I think my Irish Granny would have hit Bill with the parasol if he hadn't vamoosed.

Least ways, Granny finished her shopping, with me at her side, and we retreated up the hill.

I thought the problem between Carl and me would rear its ugly head Monday in school, but it didn't. Even though Carl had lost a little of his pizzazz on Saturday, he joked with me about losing his ice cream cone.

"The next time you swing at me, will you wait until I finish my ice cream?" Everybody laughed. Carl and I became good friends.

⌒

I can remember my father giving me lectures on sex when I was younger. Generally, a complete lecture would be forthcoming following some question I would inadvertently ask concerning sex.

For example, one day I asked my father what the word "concupiscence" meant.

"I don't know, Charlie. I've never heard of the word. Get me the dictionary." While Dad was looking up the word, I remained in thoughtful silence. I had already looked up the word, but sought some clarification.

"Charlie, where did you find this word?" I thought the question sounded sort of ominous.

"I got it out of the Bible, Dad."

"Go get your Bible and show it to me."

Using the Bible that my grandmother had given me, I turned to Colossians. The word "concupiscence" appeared in the third chapter, the fifth verse.

Dad read the verse carefully and at first said nothing.

"What is lust, Dad?"

"Charlie, the word 'lust' concerns, in your case, the feelings that you might have for a woman. I really can't say why the man who wrote this chapter used the word 'concupiscence.' Why didn't he just call it lust and be done with it?"

"Paul wrote Colossians, Dad."

"Oh, yes, Paul. Paul was the greatest of Christ's apostles."

"Have you ever felt lust for a woman, Dad?"

"Of course, Charlie. All normal men have felt lust for a woman. It's the evil lust that Paul is talking about. Your desire for a woman should be decent It should be decent and sincere."

"When is lust evil, Dad?"

"Your lust would be evil, Charlie, if you were married, for example, and felt lust for another woman who wasn't your wife. That would be adultery."

"You should never lust for a woman who isn't your wife, Dad?"

"Charlie, you don't understand. Let's put it this way. Someday you will get married to a young woman. Right now, you are only 12 years old. When you find the woman you want to marry, you will feel a healthy lust for her, but it will not be the kind of evil lust that Paul the apostle was talking about."

"Dad, what if I feel lust for more than one woman

before I get married? Would I be committing adultery with everyone except the one woman I marry?"

"Yes, Charlie. You would be committing adultery. You would be guilty of evil lust. God never intended that a man should have any more than one wife."

I had several other questions for Dad, but I could see that his patience was wearing thin, so I asked him one question that I had wanted to ask earlier.

"Dad, the other day in the barber shop, Mr. Neil asked me if I had ever loped my mule, and everybody in the barber shop laughed. What was Mr. Neil talking about?"

Grandmother was calling us to dinner, so Dad, ignoring my question, said, "Come on Charlie, let's eat."

～～～

Many times when Mitch and I retired to the shed for a smoke I could make out Uncle John through the one shed window a scant 100 feet from Uncle John's small cottage. Uncle John would be sitting in his hickory chair on the porch. He always seemed to be immobile like a statue. I wondered what he thought about while sitting all those long hours each day. "Could he be thinking about his participation in the war?" I wondered.

When I put the question to Mitch, he explained that his grandpa sits in that chair on his porch from spring until fall, most of the time, and he added thoughtfully, "If it isn't too cold or rainy." One Saturday morning, shortly after school started in the fall, Mitch and I were in the shed sawing boards to make rabbit traps. Mitch was in an especially good humor because Uncle John had given him a dollar for his birthday.

"Mitch, what are you going to buy with your dollar?" I asked with a little envy.

"I'm going to buy some tailor-made cigarettes," Mitch grinned. "I'll buy dominoes. They're only 10 cents a package. It's more fun to smoke tailor mades than it is to smoke Old Advertiser. Old Advertiser leaks in my mouth."

As I thought about Mitch's newfound wealth, I could certainly appreciate my friendship with Mitch. Mitch always shared whatever he had with me, whether it be smokes or candy. It would be great, I thought, to smoke some tailor-made cigarettes like the movie stars smoked. Mitch had mentioned to me only yesterday in school that Stewart's Store was selling Bull Durham for 5 cents a sack. A nickel was a lot easier to come by than a quarter any old day and, besides, I liked Bull Durham tobacco.

When Mitch and I were together, which was most of the time, Mitch often broached the subject of his grandfather and his seemingly endless exploits.

"I was told by Grandpa," Mitch began recounting one day, "that he was on the square in Springfield, Missouri, when Wild Bill Hickock killed a man in a gun fight."

"Did Uncle John actually see Wild Bill shoot the man?" I asked with great interest.

"Yes, he actually saw the shooting. He really saw the man that Hickock shot fall dead." And Mitch continued, "Grandpa said that Wild Bill walked over to the dead man, collected the watch he had lost to the man in the poker game, along with the money, stood for a moment studying the crowd, walked over to the livery stable for his horse, and left town." Grandpa said no one tried to stop him.

"I'll bet they didn't. Wild Bill was really fast on the draw," I added.

I well remember the trip I took to Arizona when I was only 10 years old. I was very excited about the trip because the only time I would be out of the state of Missouri or Kansas was about to take place. We didn't have much money for our sojourn west, but Dad was able to get a pass, both for himself and me. Grandmother, bless her heart, said she would prepare a large basket of food for us to take, because, as Dad had warned, eating a meal in the diner was rather expensive.

The purpose of our trip was twofold. We were going to visit Dad's brother, my Uncle Willard, whom I had never seen, and the other reason was, as Uncle Willard had noted in his last letter, the suggestion he might be able to find my dad a job in Yuma, where Uncle Willard was the station agent for the Southern Pacific Railroad. Once Dad read his brother's letter, he immediately went to the depot in Aldrich and wired Frisco headquarters for our passes. That night, Dad told me about the proposed outing, that we might be traveling to Yuma, Arizona, soon.

"Dad, I will miss school."

"I know, Charles, but if I can find a job in Yuma, we will enroll you in school out there."

For several nights in a row, I couldn't sleep. I was so excited about seeing my uncle and his family for the first time. And, as Dad had explained, I would get to see Indians and cowboys, and maybe I could pan for gold. Every day when I came home from school I would inquire of Dad about the passes. Had they come yet?

Finally, they came, and we prepared to leave.

When we boarded the train on a Saturday morning, Grandmother kissed me and waved as the train pulled out. I was headed on a fantastic journey. I thought of the Forty-Niners who left Westport headed for Oregon or California in the 1860s. This would be an adventure. I thought of the Aldrich farmer who bragged on the streets of Aldrich that he had never been out of Polk County and was proud of it. I could not share his sentiments. I wanted to see the world.

"Charles, your Uncle Willard and Jamie, his wife, are Christian Scientists. I'm telling you now so you won't embarrass them with questions. Uncle Willard and Aunt Jamie are awfully nice people. Willard was a victim of mustard gas during World War I, and he also suffers from shell shock."

"Dad, what's a Christian Scientist?"

"Charlie, a Christian Scientist doesn't believe in seeing a doctor when they are sick."

"Why not, Dad?"

"Because they believe the Lord will cure them of whatever it is that ails them. They don't believe they need doctors. They just need faith in God to get well."

For the rest of the trip, Dad and I watched the landscape go by. When we reached the mountains, I really enjoyed Dad's stories about the Old West. But there was one story that stands out in my mind.

When the train stopped in Columbus, New Mexico, Dad said to look out on the town and visualize as much of the area as I could.

"I will tell you about the happenings in Columbus in 1916, as they pertain to your Uncle Willard."

"Has Uncle Willard been in Columbus, Dad?"

"Yes, he has," Dad smiled.

"It was in November of 1916, the third year of World War I, that the infamous Mexican revolutionary Pancho Villa crossed the U.S. border and attacked the town of Columbus, New Mexico. Pancho's revolutionary army consisted of about 400 men who proceeded to terrorize the small population of Columbus for several hours, while killing eight of its citizens."

"Dad, what did Uncle Willard have to do with Pancho's raid?"

"Charlie, your Uncle Willard was on duty at the Southern Pacific depot, which you just saw a few minutes ago, when the raid occurred. When Willard first heard gunfire and saw large groups of men riding up and down the darkened streets of Columbus, he decided to lock the door of the depot and remain inside. He said he didn't have the slightest idea what was going on, but he was fairly sure that what was happening out there was none of his business. The next morning, with American Army troops guarding the town, Uncle Willard was glad for his decision to remain in the depot. He could certainly have been killed."

Besides taking eight people's lives, the bandits had burned several buildings, including the Columbus Hotel. Several citizens had been wounded in the fray. When I heard Dad's story, I made a vow I would return to that small hamlet someday and look it over carefully. I was interested in noting the American Army chased Pancho all over Mexico, seeking to punish him for his raid on the small town of Columbus. But, unfortunately, Pancho eluded his would-be captors completely. Pancho was shot to death by a rival revolutionary in the early '20s in Old Mexico.

Horace Kirby was a miser of the first rank. His stories are legend around Aldrich and Dadeville. One day an airplane descended on the little town of Aldrich, Missouri, bearing two lawyers who wanted nothing more than the signature of Horace Kirby on oil leases that would give him the status of a millionaire. There is no doubt that Horace was a millionaire before the advent of the airplane landing in Aldrich.

But let's go back to the known beginning of Horace Kirby. Horace hitchhiked to Texas as a young man, by his own admittance, and made the original stake that would propel him into the millionaire class. Namely, he stole cattle and sold them to any number of people. When he had enough money to leave the state of Texas, under duress and various other outstanding indictments, he tucked $50,000 into a red bandana handkerchief, put the ball of money at the end of a long stick and headed for Missouri. He hitchhiked all the way. When he got to Missouri, he began buying land from people who couldn't pay their taxes and loaning money to anyone and everyone who could show some collateral. Most of the Missouri rural folks, being poor, used their milk cows or team of horses to get a loan from "Uncle" Horace. Some of the people actually used their homes as collateral for loans, or their wedding ring.

Horace was good to loan money to the people who could show some collateral but was indifferent to those clients who could not meet their obligations by the date on the contract. His usual statement to those who needed more time to pay off their indebtedness was, "You made the agreement. You took my money, so you owe me thus and such." It was often repeated in the Aldrich realm that he would take the milk cow from a family with five kids if the family couldn't pay the loan off on the due date. He didn't seem to suffer any emotional distress, according to witnesses.

The first time I came in contact with the ungodly gentleman was in Osa's Cafe. My father and I went into Osa's to have Sunday dinner. Dad noted the man on our left was acting queerly, when he brought out of his hunting coat a whiskey bottle filled with milk, reached in his outer pocket and pulled out a package wrapped in stale newspaper and asked the restaurant lady, Osa, for a glass. By this time, he was being observed by the other patrons in the restaurant.

My father, being a kindly man, told Osa to give the man a meal and he would pay for it. Osa laughed at Dad's suggestion and whispered, "Ralph, that is Horace Kirby. He owns half of the county and half of several other counties, probably."

Dad acknowledged that he didn't know the gentleman.

Osa smiled as she gave the requested glass to Mr. Kirby, who sat several stools away from my father and me. Dad and I watched Mr. Kirby empty the milk from the whiskey bottle into Osa's glass. He then unwrapped the package and took out three rather large pieces of cornbread and proceeded to crumble the cornbread into the glass of milk.

"Dad, aren't his hands awfully dirty?" I asked.

"Yes, Charles," Dad said in a low tone, "but he farms for a living, so I guess he forgot to wash his hands." When Dad smiled, I was unable to tell if he was serious.

It seems that after our observance of Mr. Kirby on a Sunday of years past, we began to hear all sorts of interesting things concerning Mr. Kirby.

And then, one Sunday the "Springfield Daily News" did a story on Mr. Kirby. The story was quite long and comprehensive. I can no longer remember the entire story, but there are certain events that stand out. For example, Horace told the reporter that as he was hitchhiking back to Missouri from Texas with $50,000 wrapped in a bandana handkerchief, a hobo suggested that he and Horace cover a town for handouts. The hobo would take one side of the track and he, the other. They would meet at the railroad junction. Horace said he told the hobo friend, when they met at the junction after canvassing for food, that he didn't have any luck. But he said the hobo shared what food he had been able to panhandle.

Another engaging story concerning this 20th century "Silas Marner" took place down in the Cookson Hill country of Oklahoma. Horace owned several thousand acres in the proximity of a farm implement dealer in a small town that Horace visited one stormy spring afternoon. Horace was greeted by two or three farm folks who stood around a potbellied stove because it was really a cold, wet day. The owner of the implement company, upon observing Mr. Kirby enter his store, came out from the small office and greeted Mr. Kirby. Immediately, the store owner could see that Mr. Kirby was cold and pretty wet and he seemed to be shivering.

"Sir, I have a good coat that I never wear hanging in my office. You're sure welcome to it."

Horace thanked the man and said that he could sure use a coat.

The man soon returned with the promised coat

and handed it to Horace, who immediately put it on, thanking him again. Horace wanted to know the price of a spring tooth harrow, which brought a look of surprise to the store owner, who was now trying to be nonchalant about the whole affair. When the price was stated, Mr. Kirby didn't comment for a couple of minutes. He just stood close to the stove rubbing his hands for additional warmth.

"Sir, I would like four spring tooth harrows. Could you deliver them for me? 'Why, why, yes I could.'" Without further conversation, Horace pulled out an Old Advertiser sack, pulled the drawstring and started pulling out a wad of bills—hundred dollar bills. The store owner took the proffered money without comment. I think he must have been speechless. He had made a faux paux and didn't really understand what to do about it. Yet, he would make an effort.

"Sir, I'm sorry about the coat. I really didn't understand. I hope I didn't offend you."

Horace assured the store owner he wasn't offended, that he needed the coat.

As Horace walked out the front door, the store owner told the two men remaining by the stove that it had been a strange day. Then everyone guffawed.

Two elderly women who resided in a farm house about a quarter of a mile from Mr. Kirby's farm would take a couple of homemade pies to Horace at Christmas time. This gift of two pies at Christmas became a regular ritual. These two sweet old ladies remarked that the only response from Mr. Kirby down through the years was "thank you." And you should have heard the description of the hovel that Horace lived in. His bedroom had a dirt floor, and when the ladies took their first pies to Horace, they reported there were chickens inside his house, as well as two shoat pigs. From the road, Horace's house looked like an ancient barn that had fallen into a state of disrepair.

There are many other stories concerning this gentleman, many of which I dot not remember. The large newspaper spread that came out in the late '30s on Horace Kirby also contained many unbelievable stories that I can't recall, but what I have included in this book will give you some knowledge of Mr. Kirby.

There are a few other incidents that might interest the reader. Horace told the Springfield paper that he once stood out in a heavily weeded pasture for several hours, waiting for daylight so he could retrieve the quarter he had dropped while bringing in his grandmother's cows. He told the press that he knew he could never remember where he had dropped the quarter if he didn't stand there on the spot where he had dropped it and wait for daylight.

And by his own admittance, Horace always left the gate closed and crawled over the fence to save the hinges on the gate.

That day the small plane landed in Aldrich, the two men complained that Horace made them wait until noon to sign oil leases they had transported all the way from Tulsa, Okla., for his signature. The pilot told one of the citizens residing in Aldrich that Horace was cutting sprouts and would not stop cutting his sprouts until the noon hour, stating that he was behind in his work.

One rainy day in Aldrich, Dad told me that he had asked Mr. Kirby what he was going to do with all of his money. Horace said, "Ralph, what I would like is to have all of my wealth in cash and have it stacked up by my bed, soaked with kerosene. Just as I draw my last breath, I would like to toss a match to it."

Dad told me he couldn't understand that kind of thinking, suggesting that "Horace could do a lot of good with his money, if he were willing to do so. He is guilty of self love, Charlie. The opposite of God is self."

Horace Kirby couldn't read or write. He signed his legal papers and checks with an "X." But people who knew him said he was very astute in all of his affairs and they had never known of anyone beating him out of a dime.

The end for Horace Kirby came on a spring day in his 65th year. He had entered my beloved Sac River with a large millstone tied around his neck. I wasn't in the vicinity when they buried Horace but would have attended the funeral if I had been there.

My father said of Horace, "I don't think he understood his world very well, and that's the case of many people."

It was snowing heavily when I left the high school building after basketball practice. I was really hungry and looked forward to Granny's promised supper of cornbread and cold milk. But when I got home, Granny met me at the door and told me rather sorrowfully that my dad was in Bolivar and she didn't have the necessary 10 cents for a gallon of milk.

I told Granny that I would take Dad's shotgun and go kill a rabbit. Since it was not long until dark, I hurried to change into my old overalls, told Granny good-bye and started east of Aldrich on a snow-covered road. It was beautiful in the late afternoon, and the snow was still coming down, but not so heavily.

I was enjoying the quiet peacefulness and the dancing snowflakes. Tomorrow, I thought, would be a good day to hunt rabbits. I would probably hunt all day, and then I thought of the three shells in my pocket. I would need shells. J.C. Stewart would let me charge a box of shells, which cost 45 cents, and I could pay him for the shells the next evening when I returned from hunting. I was hoping that Roy Neil at the produce was still paying 10 cents for rabbits.

As these thoughts were running through my mind, I spied fresh rabbit tracks that led across the road and into the ditch on the north side. I slipped up to the side of the road where the rabbit tracks led into the ditch. All of a sudden, Mr. Bunny came charging out of the ditch and ran straight down the road. I killed him with a clean shot from my old Belgian double barrel.

I quickly gutted the rabbit and headed down the road to Neil's Produce, where Roy gave me a dime for the rabbit. From Neil's Produce, I made my way across the street to Stewart's Store, where J.C. charged me for a box of shells. I was now ready for Saturday's hunt. Maybe Dad would go with me if he came back from Bolivar in time. I went back up the hill to Granny's and told her I had killed a rabbit. Granny laughed and handed me the tin gallon milk bucket.

I had killed the rabbit a mere 500 yards from our house. Uncle Tom Degraffenreid's house was about a hundred yards on down the same road. Uncle Tom commented on the weather as he filled my bucket with good cold milk.

Granny and I had an excellent supper of cornbread and cold milk topped with a piece of gooseberry pie.

The best place to loaf and meet other loafers was, of course, Osa's Cafe, the only restaurant in Aldrich. There were a few attempts, from time to time, to start another restaurant, but Osa's Cafe was the last word and survived until Aldrich ended as a town with the coming of Stockton Lake. Osa was a swell lady who was sometimes generous to a fault. How she put up with all of us guys is a mystery.

The nickelodeon in Osa's restaurant contained mostly hillbilly songs, as I recall. One day, Marion and I had purchased a Coke from Osa and were perusing the new records which had just been added that day. I noticed one of the new songs was "South of the Border," sung by Dennis Day, a radio actor on the Jack Benny show. When Mitch said he had one nickel to play the machine, he asked me what my choice was. I told him I would like to hear "South of the Border."

When Dennis began to sing, I said, "That guy's a really good singer." There were six or eight other people in Osa's who were listening to the Dennis Day record. One such person informed me the music was too "high falutin,'" and I answered the charge by stating that Dennis doesn't sing through his nose.

"That's opera," the protagonist said flatly.

I answered the second charge by advising the young gentleman he wouldn't know opera from sheep manure.

Osa laughed, and Mitch and I left and went to his shed to work on some box traps I had found in the Stewart woods.

When J.C. Stewart, later Colonel Stewart, asked me

if I had taken his box traps, I answered in the affirmative and further explained they had been there for years and I had surmised they were abandoned. J.C. laughed.

"Charlie," he said, "you can have the traps, but you should have asked me." I agreed and found a great friend.

I always seemed to have misgivings when the yuletide season approached, partly because poverty always seemed to lie heavily on the land. The only Xmas trees or Xmas decorations visible in Aldrich were to be found in the grade school and high school or in the churches. I don't remember anyone dressing up as Santa Clause in Aldrich. But I can say that when the word Christmas was written, no one used "Xmas." Everyone wrote the full word because Xmas was celebrated as the birthday of Christ. When I told Dad that a book I read declared Xmas to be a pagan holiday, he declared that Jesus Christ was the son of God and that Jesus was not a pagan. When I thought about the word pagan, it troubled me, but I soon forgot the article and accepted Dad's explanation.

I lived with Sara seven years. I don't recall Granny ever receiving a Christmas present, and the same goes for my father. We never had a Christmas tree during my days in Aldrich. I did hint to Dad once that we find a Christmas tree in the woods and bring it home. Dad promptly vetoed the idea, stating that we didn't have decorations for a tree. I lamely suggested that Grandmother could pop some corn to string on the tree. Dad ignored my suggestion.

I can still remember vividly the annual Christmas

programs held each year in the Aldrich High School gymnasium. All of us guys knew the merchants would give out sacks of candy that contained an orange, some nuts and a small assortment of hard candies, buttressed by two or three bell-shaped chocolates. This sack of candy would, in many cases, represent all of the Christmas many of my friends would get. I shared my Christmas candy with Dad and Granny.

After the Christmas program was over one year, Zelma Toalson, the grocer, began his custom of handing out sacks of candy. When he got to Mitch and me, we could see that he had handed out the last sack to the boy who sat on our right. I'm sure Zelma must have seen our crestfallen look.

"We've run out of candy," he remarked pleasantly, smiling. He bent over Marion and me and said, "You and Marion go with me to the store, and I will get you guys your candy." Needless to say, Zelma was as good as his promise and gave Mitch and me a much larger portion of candy than the rest of the kids had received. I was ecstatic with my sack that contained five bell-shaped chocolates.

Another situation that gave me a feeling of melancholy was that I couldn't visit my Granny Birt and my brother, Nelson, in Kansas City. A bus ticket was, as I remember, $6 roundtrip. But $6 was a lot of money.

Getting back to school, in the grade school we were able to make our family simple Christmas presents. But in high school, we exchanged presents by the name we had drawn out of Mr. Cavender's box. These exchange gifts had to be purchased. I remember Berniece Rotrock being handed an elegantly packaged gift from her boyfriend who had drawn her name. When she unwrapped the beautiful package, it contained a snow-white slop jar. Everyone in the study hall roared with laughter. In case you are wondering what a slop jar is, it's a portable toilet made for communities that had all their toilets outside.

Christmas was much different in the 1930s in schools across the land. For example, our Christmas convocation featured all sorts of music, including many religious songs. At least two Protestant ministers would address the student body, followed by a prayer. I can say with absolute certainty that the ACLU was not consulted concerning the Aldrich School convocation, nor was the U.S. Supreme Court. Also, we did not hear Bing Crosby singing "I'm Dreaming of a White Christmas." The song hadn't been written yet.

Since youth is eternally optimistic, I can readily tell everyone that I enjoyed the Christmas holidays. I was able to run my 40 boxtraps every morning, plus steel traps I had set on Sac River for muskrats and mink and coons. After I had run my trap line, I would often hunt rabbits the rest of the day. If I shot a rabbit with my 12-gauge, the shell cost 3 cents. So every time I killed a rabbit, I made 7 cents.

Finally, I always dreaded the question, "Charlie, what did you get for Christmas?"

I wouldn't ask any of my friends that question, and I always hoped no one would ask me.

Merry Christmas!

❧

There were other tidbits my father remembered after we made his tapes. These extra tidbits require only a few paragraphs for the telling. As Dad introduced me to these interesting anecdotes, I was determined to include them in my manuscript. The reader can be the judge of their worth.

Ed Davis lived on a farm about three miles north of Aldrich. One day Ed was plowing his corn on the north 40. It was a glorious spring day in the year 1910. Ed, walking slowly behind his team of horses, watched the furrows unfold in the thick black loam. All of a sudden, Ed heard a terrible noise behind him. Glancing back toward the north, Ed beheld a graf zepplin, grayish in the afternoon sun and huge, coming directly at him. Now Ed was not aware that the Germans were building zepplins. Nor was he aware that the Germans were crossing the Atlantic in their zepplins. In fact, Ed did not know there was such an animal. So, dropping the reins to his horses, with his straw hat in his hand, Ed ran screaming toward his farm house, where his wife was busily engaged in her garden. Screaming as loud as he could, "Ma, get in the house. The world is coming to an end!" Both Ed and his wife ran inside their kitchen and into the pantry where they tried to catch their breath. When the terrible noise subsided, and that is the way the Davis family described the zepplin's noise, they came out of the pantry and surveyed the sky, but the zepplin was out of sight. Ed could still see his horses standing in the field, where he had dropped the reins.

Dad made the remark that Ed was not fond of the zepplin story when he came to Aldrich on Saturday to do his trading. He did tell one group of loafers in front of Stewart's Store, who had displayed a scornful attitude.

"You'da been scared, too, if you'da been there."

My father was hired by the Frisco Railroad as a telegrapher in his 16th year, 1917, the third year of World War I in Europe. His first job was in Stanley, Kan. Upon arriving there, he entered into a boarding agreement with a family of eight, whose house was close to the depot. There were no hotels in the small town of Stanley.

Dad said that within a few days of his arrival in Stanley, the mother of the family he was staying with contracted the Spanish flu, or influenza. In a matter of days, her children also came down with the Spanish flu. Within two weeks, Dad said all six children died, along with the mother. The father of this family was the only one to survive.

And then Dad contracted the flu and took to his bed in his boarding house with a high fever. He had left instructions with his replacement not to notify his mother that he was ill. The man ignored his request and sent a message on the wire for Granny that her son had the flu and a high fever.

Granny caught the afternoon train and was "Johnny on the Spot" with her medical kit. Upon her arrival, she gave Dad a strong purgative or cathartic. The next morning, Dad's fever had broken, and Dad was well on the road to recovery.

Years later, I read that the Spanish flu had killed more than 20 million people through the world. I remember that my uncles Birt and Rob told of seeing corpses at Camp Funston in Fort Riley, Kan., during their stay there, stacked like cord wood. It was terribly cold, and the young soldiers were dying faster than the Army could bury them.

I remember reading somewhere that you don't have to deserve your mother's love; you have to deserve your father's love because fathers are more particular. Mothers will love you in spite of who you are or what you do. Granny Dickerson could have caught the Spanish flu when she made her trip to Stanley, but I'm sure she never gave it a thought. Granny was a saint in my book.

<hr>

True, there were exciting things going on in the 1930s. Lots of people were getting their chickens stolen, and guys like "Machine Gun" Kelly and John Dillinger were out there somewhere robbing banks. Every now and then I would read an article in the Springfield paper concerning some escapade of Bonnie and Clyde or Pretty Boy Floyd. But these people and their exploits seemed far removed from the bucolic setting of Aldrich.

The awareness of a terrible Depression was pretty much understood by most of the people in Aldrich, although the causes of the Depression seemed to present a multiplicity of confusion. Sam Hughes, a local sage, said the bankers were responsible for the Depression, while Henry Perkins, the town barber, said the Depression was caused by the Democrats and that damn cripple, Franklin Roosevelt, who was spending us into bankruptcy. Politics seemed to furnish the principal topic of discussion for the loafers who sat day after day in front of Stewart's Hardware Store or up at Roy Neil's Produce House or wherever they could find a place to sit out of the sun. Some of the good old boys claimed the rich had all the money. But life went on, and the Depression deepened, and I listened when I could.

I liked the old Spanish proverb that stated "It's so lovely to do nothing, and then rest afterward." I don't know what made me think of that. Perhaps it was the Aldrich loafers sitting out the day.

Only yesterday, Mitch had announced that "[Lawrence] of Arabia" had been killed. This was a blow to both of us because we looked upon Lawrence as one of the World's great heroes. We had both read his book, The Seven Pillars of Wisdom.

"How was he killed, Mitch?"

"The paper said he was riding his motorcycle down a country lane and ran off the road trying to dodge another vehicle. It was just a short article."

I remember that Mitch had purchased a secondhand motorcycle soon after he found out that Lawrence of Arabia was a motorcycle buff. He had some difficulty in persuading me to ride with him. A big Harley on gravel roads seemed a mite dangerous for a novice.

Mitch and I acquired several heroes during the eight years that I spent in Aldrich. When Wiley Post and Will Rogers were killed in Alaska, we mourned their loss. Aviation was exciting to both of us, much more than the motorcycle. We spent many hours discussing flying and airplanes. We tried to see every movie that came along that concerned flying. Earlier, we had constructed a mock airplane by using a ladder with two missing rungs, which gave us room to sit down in the ladder that was propped up on two sawhorses. We used large paint buckets to sit on, and fashioned an instrument panel out of cardboard. We spent many wonderful hours flying our mock plane all over the country. But, to youth, repetition soon becomes a burden, so we abandoned the idea of flying, and turned to other boyhood dreams.

Our interest in flying was quickly renewed, though, when a small plane landed in Aldrich, south of town. All the youngsters in town surrounded the airplane, and some of the guys were trying to get in the cockpit. The two gentlemen, one of whom was flying the plane, was rather curt in telling the youth of Aldrich not to touch the airplane and, in a more compromising voice, wanted to know where Horace Kirby lived. One of the several adults that ventured out to see the plane was advised by one of the two gentlemen that he was needing to contact Horace Kirby to sign some papers. The Horace Kirby story has already been told in this book.

One spring morning, I walked down the hill and joined Mitch in his shed, or "workshop" as he was wont to call it. Mitch was having a Bull Durham cigarette and laughed as I picked up the bag of tobacco and said, "I don't mind if I do."

I was startled at Mitch's next remark:

"Dick, did you know that Grandpa has hired your dad to stay with him at night?"

"No, Mitch, when did you learn this?"

"Grandpa told me this morning when I was filling his kindling box. He said Ralph Dickerson was going to stay with him starting next week."

"How much will he pay Dad, Mitch?"

"He didn't say. The only thing he mentioned was he needed some company, and I reckon he does. He's too feeble to walk uptown anymore. The only time anyone comes to visit him, other than you and me, or Mother, is when some of the gamblers in town come to play poker with him. They don't really come to visit; they just want to win his money," Marion said stiffly.

I glanced through the workshop window and observed Uncle John sitting in his cane chair. I was glad Dad was going to stay with him. I was soon to discover Dad's salary would be four dollars per week. Four dollars was a lot of money in the early '30s. Cigarettes were 10 cents a package, while Bull Durham was a nickel a sack. Cokes, candy bars and hamburgers were 5 cents, to give you some idea of the worth of a dollar.

As the weeks slipped by, Dad would sometimes impart bits of interesting conversation that he had picked up from Uncle John. Dad had several times remarked that Uncle John possessed a good mind.

One Saturday, Dad informed me at the breakfast table that the Katy Railroad in Kansas City had notified him of a possible job as a Rate Clerk, and that he was to appear at their Main Office the following Monday in Kansas City. This was exciting news for all of us, including Granny. Dad had been without a job for several years.

"Charlie," he said, "you can stay with Uncle John while I'm gone. That way, we won't lose our small income," Dad laughed.

Dad had gone to Kansas City, and I walked down the hill toward Uncle John's house in the early evening. I had promised Dad that I would get there before dark. As I approached the lane leading down past Mitch's house, I could see Uncle John sitting in his accustomed chair on the front porch. He always appeared to be a statue, from a distance, never seeming to move.

When I got within a few feet of Uncle John, I said "hello." His facial demeanor seemed to express a certain pleasantness at my greeting, but of this, I could not be certain. I had not presented myself to Uncle John as a visitor for several weeks. I was glad that the old gentlemen seemed to be congenial, since I would be spending the next few nights with him.

As the threat of war had intensified, I often thought of Uncle John and wondered if he knew what was happening. I knew that he didn't have a radio and couldn't see well enough to read the Springfield paper. During my infrequent visitations with him in the past, it had become obvious that he was not very cognizant of what was happening in Europe. "I have come to stay with you, sir. Dad is in Kansas City, seeing about a job."

"Ralph told me yesterday," Uncle John said simply. "Sit down, boy." I sat down in the cane chair and noticed that Uncle John was looking at me rather questionably.

"When will your dad be back?" The question was unexpected.

"I don't know, sir," I answered truthfully, remembering that Dad had not mentioned the date of his return. I waited for some further conversation from Uncle John, but only silence ensued. I could hear a chorus of tree frogs and observed the lightning bugs making their appearance in the deepening twilight.

I glanced at Uncle John, wondering when he would say something. He sat rather rigid, looking straight ahead. I could no longer make out his countenance because of the darkness. The black hat he always wore outside partly obscured his face. Summer lightning was becoming more prominent in the southern sky, and the chorus of tree frogs seemed to increase in intensity. I was getting sleepy and looked forward to sleeping on the cot that had been prepared for Dad, but which I would occupy this night. I suddenly asked Uncle John to tell me a story. He had told me several stories over the years, so my request was natural, for his stories always were about the Civil War.

Uncle John seemed to ponder my request, slowly stroking his goatee. His pale blue eyes looked tired, I thought, and a little impatient. Uncle John shuffled his feet, gently tapping his cane against the hickory chair. I thought that he probably didn't hear me. Then, he turned again and gazed directly at me.

"Boy, would you fix me a toddy?" he asked in a whisper.

"What's the matter, sir, don't you feel well?"

"No, boy, I feel all right, I just need a toddy to help me sleep." I remembered that Dad had told me how to prepare a toddy for Uncle John.

"He don't drink very often, Charlie," Dad had explained, "but you make him a toddy if he asks for it."

I immediately went inside to the small kitchen and lit the coal oil stove, mixing a shot glass of whiskey into the hot water. When I handed Uncle John his toddy, he thanked me in a low voice. He drank the toddy slowly.

"You should never drink, son," he said softly.

I sat quietly, admiring the full moon that brightened the summer night. It would be a good night to fish from the overflow bridge south of town. Dad and I were planning on going fishing when he got the notice to come to Kansas City about a job. I hoped that Dad would get the job. He had been mostly broke for so long.

When Uncle John finished his toddy, his somnolent bearing seemed to change. He sat straight up in his hickory chair and gazed at me.

"Boy, did I ever tell you about working a cattle roundup in Western Kansas," he paused, "after the war was over?"

"No!" I exclaimed.

"I think the year was 1880, or around that time," Uncle John began. "I was working for a cattle company, branding cattle for different ranchers in the area."

When I heard Uncle John's story introduction, I immediately took on an air of indifference because I wanted to hear stories about the Civil War. I was not interested in cattle drives. But, I affirmed to Uncle John, "No, you have never told me that story."

Uncle John seemed pleased by my remark and began his story.

"I think the year was 1880 or around that time. I was working with about twenty other cowhands. We generally ate our supper of beans and beef around the campfire, after dark. Men who had spent most of their daylight hours in the saddle usually retired to their bedrolls soon after supper."

Uncle John stopped and stared into the night.

"Boy, what's that noise I hear?"

I could hear a chorus of hounds that sounded like they were coming up the river, west of Aldrich. I figured they were Ralph Coffman's hounds chasing a fox.

"Uncle John, you hear foxhounds. I think the hounds are chasing a fox."

Uncle John's expression did not change. He seemed satisfied with my explanation and continued with his story.

"On this particular night, ten or twelve of the cowhands filled their coffee cups and gathered around the cook's campfire after finishing their supper. I joined the men around the fire and listened to the men as they joshed one another. Then, one of the men told about his experiences in the war, a very interesting story that seemed to draw the group a little closer together. Soon, others began to contribute to the entertainment by relating a story or happening. Most of the stories I heard that evening concerned the Civil War, or the Great Rebellion, depending on who was telling the story. I couldn't tell whether any man telling his story had fought for the North or the South."

"Did you really care, Uncle John?" I asked with some interest. Uncle John looked at me, showing what I took to be impatience. He seemed to be uncomfortable. I waited for his answer. I was almost ready to ask the question again, when Uncle John replied:

"I guess I didn't care too much boy. But you must understand that even fifteen or twenty years after the war, most people in the North and South had strong feelin's about who was on which side."

"Uncle John, did the North think that God was on their side?"

"Yes, boy, I think they did, but so did the South. Lincoln prayed to God many times for victory. Jeff Davis prayed to the same God for victory for the South."

"God couldn't give both a victory, could He?"

Uncle John ignored my question and, after a long pause, resumed his story.

"I started to tell my story by informing my compadres that I joined the Union Army when I was 15 years old. I was taken into the Eighth Iowa Calvary as a horse soldier. My first engagement, the first time I saw a Southern Rebel, was in the Battle of Nashville in 1863. At the time of the Battle of Nashville, I was barely 16."

"You were awfully young to be a soldier," I suggested. "Were there a lot of young guys like you in the Northern Army?"

"Yes, boy, lots of the soldiers were barely in their teens."

"Well, anyway," Uncle John said, "three or four out of the group of cowhands who were listening to my story volunteered to remark that they, too, had fought in the Battle of Nashville." With no comment from me, Uncle John paused.

I was hoping that he would finish his story before he went in to retire for the night. While I was at this point of conjecture, Uncle John continued.

"I remember General Johnson's Rebel Army was retreating south toward Nashville, Tennessee. General Buell, the Northern commander of the Second Corps, and my commanding officer, was pushing Johnson in his retreat."

My flagging interest in Uncle John's story was revived. I was going to hear a good Civil War story! Uncle John continued.

"In the afternoon an order came down the line to pull up and make camp or bivouac. I figured that the attack on Johnson's army would not take place until tomorrow at daybreak. I had spotted a stream not too far back of our present line and, after checking with my fellow comrades, I mounted my horse and rode north toward the stream. After a short ride around a heavily forested area, I came out on a hillside. Below me, I saw a valley that contained the stream I was looking for. A cursory glance toward the valley showed no evidence of rebel soldiers, nor was there any sign of human habitation.

Putting my horse into a gallop, I rode down the valley toward the stream, noticing as I did so that the other side of the stream was pretty heavily forested with large trees. The meadow that I had ridden through had probably been farmed sometime in the past. As I surveyed the stream for a place to bathe, I kept my eye on the thick growth of trees on the far side of the stream.

"My first thought was that the trees could hide a company of rebels without my seeing them. I noticed a hole of water that was of ample depth for my bath, with a gravel bar that bordered the stream. I decided that I would take a quick bath and get back to my comrades. I took off my uniform pants and boots, disrobed hurriedly, and waded into the stream. I then jumped into the deeper water to rid myself of the soap lather. The water was so clear that I opened my eyes. When I did, I observed a brownish-colored box lying on the bottom of the stream. I quickly did another shallow dive, for the water was no more than six feet deep at its deepest point, and, this time, I could see the box clearly. On my third dive, I pushed the box slightly toward the shallows on the north side of the stream. The box seemed to be very heavy and moved grudgingly. After two or three more dives, I was in a position to get the box out of the water, but, as I came up for some air, I heard the bugles sounding recall. I hurriedly dressed and rode back to my outfit. I have always wondered what was in that box, gentlemen.

"A fellow by the name of George Nixon, who sat just across the fire from me, spoke up."

"John, I can tell you what was in that box."

There was a stunned silence.

"I was astounded at the young cowhand's remark. I thought he was probably jesting, and asked laughingly,

'George, what was in the box?'

"George answered with noticeable sincerity, 'John, I was hid in a hollow sycamore tree about thirty yards from where you were swimming.' I noticed that all of the cowhands were listening carefully to George's story.

"George continued: 'The box contained my family's total wealth. There were gold coins, Confederate bonds, paper money, silverplate and stuff like that. I didn't see Grandpa prepare the box, but he told me he put everything of value in the box for me to hide because he knew the Yankees were coming.'

"Were you guarding the box, George? Is that what you were doing?"

"'Yes, John, I was to be responsible for the safety of all the valuables in the box. In fact, it was me that decided to hide the box in the stream. When you came out of the water that day, I knew that you had found the box. I had my squirrel rifle cocked and was going to kill you. But, I heard the bugles sound recall and figured you would leave, and you did. I was so glad I didn't have to shoot you!'

"I laughed and said, 'I, too, am glad you didn't shoot me, George!'

"'I was within five seconds of shooting you, John. The bugles saved your life.'

"Were you a good shot, George?"

"'Yes, John, I was an excellent shot for my years.'

"How old were you then?

"'I was 15 years old.'

"I glanced at our compadres, who were listing intently.

"Where was your father, George? Was he around your home?

"'No, John, my father was a sergeant in General Johnson's army.

"I asked: 'Did you know I was a Union soldier, George?'

"'Yes, sir, I saw your blue uniform.'

"Did you see General Buel's army when it passed through your area?

"'Yes, John, I was hiding in my hollow tree. But, your army passed mostly to the east of where I was hiding.'

"Where was your home, George? I didn't see many signs of human habitation after I left our bivouac area that day."

"George told me that his house was not visible from the valley that contained the stream, that the house was situated on a ridge, overlooking the valley. I looked at George carefully, studying his blond features. I knew that he was being truthful when he said he knew what was in the box. I was also sure that I could have died that fall day, of a squirrel rifle ball. As I think back, George couldn't have missed me from his hiding place in the hollow sycamore tree."

Uncle John looked at me slowly and said, "But fate allowed me to live many more years, about seventy-five more years."

He smiled and said, "Charles, it's my bedtime."

The moon had almost disappeared, and the summer lightning was still prevalent in the Southern sky. It had been a good evening for me and Uncle John.

❧

Clarence Alden, the Frisco station agent in Aldrich, and an admitted ventriloquist, related the following story to

Dad while night-fishing on the Sac River.

Clarence began his story by telling Dad that he was working at the main Frisco station in Springfield where all passengers disembarked. The year was 1924, he thought. On this particular day, Clarence said he noticed several well-dressed Negro men who appeared to be waiting the arrival of the Frisco Florida Special, a passenger train that was due momentarily. Sure enough, when the Florida Special pulled into the station, the group of Negro men made its way down the station platform toward the baggage car. Two railroad employees on the Florida Special opened the car door and started unloading a casket. The group of Negro men pressed forward as they watched the casket being placed on the railroad wagon.

As this procedure was taking place, a hearse pulled up to the station platform a short distance away. The railroad men, noticing the hearse, pushed the wagon containing the casket up to the back of the hearse. As the two railroad men began the transfer of the casket to the hearse, Clarence said he threw his voice at the casket, saying in a low voice, "Let me down easy, boys." The two Negro railroad employees who were engaged in loading the casket dropped their load and ran off some distance, leaving the casket's front end in the hearse, while the back of the casket sat on the ground. The group of negro mourners who had cleared the area rapidly were standing about thirty yards away, staring in wonderment.

Clarence said the Negroes began to gravitate slowly toward the rear, talking all the while in low monotones. The two baggage workers, emboldened by the proximity of the mourners, walked slowly up to the hearse, lifted up the back end of the casket, and pushed it into the hearse.

Clarence said he didn't have the heart to say anything else as he watched the hearse pull away.

Ed Davis liked to go coon hunting at night with his hound dogs. The darker the night, the better. One of Ed's favorite hunts was to make his way down the Coffman Branch until it reached Sac River. From there, Ed would follow the Sac west toward Califord Hollow and beyond. The bluff that closely followed Sac River west was, in places, pretty high. It was in the area of the high bluffs in Califord Hollow that Ed had a rather comical experience.

Missouri coon hunters in 1915 did not enjoy the luxury of flashlights. The only way a coon hunter could light up the dark night was his coal oil lantern, which didn't put out much light.

On this particular night, Ed was hunting in the Califord area with a friend who often accompanied Ed on his hunting trips. The dogs started barking treed, and Ed told his friend, who was carrying the lantern, to remain at the top of the bluff.

"I'll slide down the bluff to see if I can find the dogs." Using the lighted lantern as a point of reference, Ed made his way through some scrub brush.

All of a sudden, his companion at the top of the bluff heard Ed scream. It seems that Ed had made a misstep and started to fall but was able to grab a limb. Holding on for dear life, Ed was screaming he couldn't hold on much longer.

"Tell my wife farewell, tell my children farewell. Tell them all farewell," he shouted. And then there was silence.

Not knowing what had happened, his companion started in the direction of Ed's cries. Almost immediately Ed burst out of the brush and exclaimed that he had almost fallen. He then admitted to his companion that he had fallen about three feet and hit the ground. His companion, instead of performing a rescue operation, enjoyed a good laugh all the way home.

Needless to say, Ed's hunting companion told a number of people in Aldrich what had happened to Ed, and they laughed, too.

Afterwards, every time the dunce happened to see Ed on the streets of Aldrich, he would holler, "Farewell. Farewell. Tell them all farewell." And then Dad said the dunce would run like hell, because old Ed was a vengeful man.

One morning while running my muskrat water traps in the Sac River Bottoms, I was privileged to run into Fletch Davis, who was checking on some of his cattle. I didn't know his name, but he immediately introduced himself and wanted to know my name. When I told him, he asked me if I was having any luck with my trapping. I showed him the one muskrat I had caught, and that bit of information brought on a friendly conversation, with Mr. Davis doing most of the talking. He told me that he sometimes preached at the Pleasant Ridge Church where my mother and most of my family are buried.

I immediately seized the opportunity of inquiring how he had decided to become a preacher. I had always wondered about preachers.

Mr. Davis laughed pleasantly and proceeded to tell me that one afternoon while he was plowing his corn, the Lord called him to preach. "I was flabbergasted by the good Lord's message, and during my conversation with the Lord that day, some 30 years ago, I notified the Lord that I had only gone to the eighth grade in school, that I was dumb, in matter of fact, too dumb to be a preacher. The Lord apparently disagreed with me." And Mr. Davis laughed again, most pleasantly. I explained that I had been saved in the Methodist Church in Aldrich when I was 16 years old and I attended the Methodist Church on Sunday, as well as Ralph Taylor's Sunday School class. I waited for Mr. Davis to comment on what I had just divulged to him.

"Charles, I am so glad to make your acquaintance and to learn that you are a Christian. You should know and understand that the most important thing in your life is Jesus Christ." And with the remark, Fletch Davis shook my hand and headed down the river to his cattle.

When I told Dad of my chance encounter with Fletch Davis, he said he never had the opportunity to hear Mr. Davis preach but that he had heard some good things about his preaching.

∽

Back in the early '30s, my father was urging me to read books. One day, Dad mentioned an interesting trilogy concerning the French Foreign Legion. I checked out *Beau Geste* from the high school library. The author was Percival Wren. I was fascinated by his writing and soon read the other two books in the trilogy.

I told Marion about the trilogy and suggested that

he might want to read them. Marion was always telling me about some book he had read and he thought I would like. When Marion completed the trilogy, we entertained ourselves on rainy afternoons by discussing the French Foreign Legion. We were also very interested in Lawrence of Arabia.

Zane Grey and Peter B. Kyne were some of our favorite authors, as well as James Oliver Curwood. One story we talked about endlessly was Robert Louis Stevenson's *Kidnapped*. We were interested in anyone searching for treasure, even Huck Finn and Tom Sawyer. Marion and I enjoyed *Julius Caesar* and *The Three Musketeers*.

Even in our hillbilly setting, we were able to read quite a few books. I don't think many people in Aldrich read books. And I remember many of the books we read were deemed frivolous by our high school English teacher.

During my Aldrich tenure I found it very difficult in a Depression economy to raise money for such things as Snickers, Cokes, and, above all, the necessary funds for attending the movie that was shown every Monday night in the red barn. True, the charge for the movie was only 10 cents, but 10 cents was an indomitable fund during the '30s. Marion did not have the problem of gaining 10 cents for the red barn movie, simply because his mother owned the red barn, the so-called building that housed the Perkin's Feed Store on the first floor.

Now I want you to understand that I was no bird brain in this struggle for spendable capital. I decided to sell cloverine salve—the salve that cured almost anything. Cloverine salve cost a quarter. My take, if per chance I sold one tin of salve, was 5 cents. Finding the sale of cloverine salve growing more impossible, I switched to being the Aldrich representative for the Saturday Evening Post and the Grit newspaper. These endeavors, too, in time proved to be very unprofitable. But, being an entrepreneur of sorts, I became aware of the fact that, out of 150 million people in the United States, 15 million people were unemployed. This discouraging figure made me take a hard look at the citizens of Aldrich. I really didn't know of anyone who was gainfully employed with a full-time job, unless it was the banker. No wonder there was no market for the Saturday Evening Post or the Grit newspaper.

You should know, if you don't already, that the 1930s was a very unique time. The United States was suffering from the worst depression in its history. In the village of Aldrich, almost everyone was poor, with two or three notable exceptions. There was the banker, who lived at the bottom of the big hill below Sara's cottage. When my friends and I were bobsledding down the big hill, I always remembered admiring the well-lighted interior of the banker's home. His home was so beautiful on a night when the snow was falling. By contrast, I thought of Sara's copper wire and the many nights I spent reading by a coal oil lamp. The copper wire I am referring to was inserted into the meter to keep the wattage at a minimum. Sara would tell me that the dollar minimum charged by the electric company was all she could afford. That was the only dishonest thing Sara did in all the years I knew her. She was a saint. I can also say with complete confidence that a great many of the citizens in Aldrich practiced using the copper wire. I am amazed the man who came to read the meter did not discover these acts of larceny. Perhaps he did discover some copper wire being used, but if he did, we never heard about it.

The mail carrier in Aldrich was also thought of as rich because he purchased a new car about every two years. I can remember rushing out of Stewart's Store one night when someone in the store said the mail carrier was passing down the main street in his new car. He had a sparkling new 1936 Chevrolet that probably cost about $600. Most Aldrich citizens figured you were rich if you could spend $600 for an automobile.

At this time in the history of the United States, the country was besieged by what the papers called the "havenots." Many people who fit in the category of the unemployed were included in this category. Generally, though, the pundits who wrote about his social tragedy were talking about the millions of people who did not have the proper sustenance. Remember, there was no such thing as welfare. True, there were county poor homes, or poor houses, as they were called. There were also county agencies that helped. And, of course, the churches helped, also, but there was no welfare to be had. I remember the early calls made by the drafting boards across the country. One report in the Kansas City Star stated that there were more than 2 million young men between the ages of 19 and 21 who were unable to pass the minimum physical exam for the Army. I have often thought this lack of sustenance was the cause of so many young men failing their physical tests. I can say with certainty that I did not have enough milk to drink during my formative years, even though hand-skimmed milk was only 10 cents a gallon. A glass of cold milk was a superb treat. I can still hear Granny telling me at supper to take large bites of cornbread and to sip my milk because we don't have much milk.

During the '30s, Adolph Hitler was appearing on

the international scene. As a young lad, I would sorta hang around groups of loafers in front of Stewart's Store, listening to their discussions of Mr. Hitler. One Day, Sam Hughes stated that most of the people are Germans, anyway, so let the Germans take Czechoslovakia. Hitler is just a big bluff, Sam continued. Germany is across the ocean, so what Germany does in Europe will have no effect on the people of Polk County, Missouri. "You can bank on that," he said, "most assuredly."

So I listened to the street palaver and wondered. And then one day as I was listening to one of the good old boys castigating Franklin Roosevelt, I was amused that another Aldrich citizen spoke up and reminded the good old boy that he still has his farm, thanks to FDR. "If FDR hadn't loaned you some money, you would have lost your damn farm. Hell, boy, you're biting the hand that feeds you." Amid the guffaws and cursing, I wondered if the two gentlemen were going to mix it up. But they didn't.

I can remember my father discussing the anti-German feeling that encompassed our country during World War I.

"Charlie, the anti-German feeling was so immense in the United States that several Germans were killed, some were driven from their homes. They lost their jobs, and in some areas German families had to leave a town or area because their safety was in jeopardy."

"What caused the American people to be so cruel, Dad?"

"Charlie, it was partly propaganda. For example, pictures of a German soldier holding his sword straight up with a baby impaled on it were being circulated in the American press. This happened during the invasion of Belgium. The German High Command had asked the country of Belgium for permission to march through their country for the purpose of attacking France. Germany promised that reparations would be paid to Belgium for any damage the German Army might incur. The Belgians, honoring the mutual non-agression pact they had with France, said no to the German proposal. Germany replied that they would cross Belgium with their armies without Belgium's permission. Belgium leaders said to the Germans, 'We know we cannot stop the German onslaught, for we are a small country. But we can promise you that you will bleed every step of the way.'"

In the spring of 1935, I was becoming nervous about my upcoming eighth grade graduation. My reason for being nervous was rather practical. My only attire for the graduation exercises, which would be held in the high school gym, was a new pair of Big Smith overalls and a gray work shirt. The only shoes I could muster for this event was a pair of Brogan shoes that were pretty much worn out.

As the month of May approached, I became more apprehensive. My father knew of my predicament, but had said nothing. I knew he didn't have any funds to rectify my problem, nor did he have any way of obtaining funds. The future became so bleak that I finally told Dad that I wasn't going to the eighth grade graduation. Tearfully, I explained that I would not walk out on the stage in front of all those people in a pair of overalls and rundown shoes.

"Charlie, I know, I know," he said and put his arms

around me. "I've been thinking about your graduation. I realize that the clothes you have are inadequate, but we'll do something. Don't give up the ship."

Dad's words did little to relieve my anxiety. As the graduation exercises grew closer, I began to contemplate running away. Where would I go? I wasn't sure, but I would remove myself from the scene, at least until the graduation was over. The more I thought about running away to preserve my dignity, the more questions arose. I could go spend my time away from the scene in a cave that I knew of on Sac River, or I could go to the old haunted house that was located in deep woods about two miles east of Aldrich.

On the way home from school, I was busily engaged in mulling over my options. Dad greeted me at the door, and asked me how school had gone. I said, "Fine." Dad was smiling.

"Charlie, I talked to your grandmother in Kansas City on the phone. I told her about your lack of nice clothes for graduation. She replied that she was sorry for not realizing your lack of clothes sooner. She informed me that she and Grandpa Birt would be down this weekend to get you some new clothes. Isn't that great?"

"Yes, Dad, that's great. I'm really thrilled. How is Nelse?"

"Your grandmother didn't say, but she was very concerned about your predicament. Maybe they will bring Nelse with them. It wouldn't hurt for him to miss a couple of school days." I agreed and hoped Nelse would come, too.

When Mother died in 1930 of Spinal Meningitis, Nelson went to live with Granny Birt, our grandmother.

I went to live in Aldrich with Granny Dickerson, our

dad's mother. Dad was on the so-called extra board when Mother died, working as a telegrapher for the Frisco Railroad part-time, as agencies needed him. We lived in Kansas City on Michigan Avenue, where I attended a very large grade school with hundred of students. When I left the city to go live with my Grandmother Dickerson, I was shocked at the difference in Kansas City and Aldrich. My costume of knickers hardly drew a comment in the city school. But, in Aldrich, knickers were so different from what the average lad was wearing; in fact, if you had knickers on, your were subject to a fist fight. I know because it was me who opined for Big Smith overalls.

When I told Nelse of my early dilemma, he laughed. But, at the time, buster, it was no laughing matter. I felt worse than the "Outcast of Poker Flat."

I missed my brother and loved him very much, but I was glad he could live in Kansas City where he could live in a nice home, and have a bicycle. I really didn't get to see Nelse too often, since he and I were both in school. The summers presented opportunities for good visits, though.

The words of Grandfather Birt talking to my father the previous summer came back to me.

"Ralph," he had said, "I don't even know there is a depression unless I read it in the paper, or maybe see a group of people in a soup line."

Dad had exclaimed that W.J.'s position was amazing and wanted to know how much the Katy Railroad paid him.

"Ralph," he had answered, "I draw $220 every fifteen days."

"Good Lord, W.J., that's a lot of money. My last job as

a telegrapher paid six dollars a day."

Later, Dad told me that W.J. was the Chief Engineer on the Fast Katy Special, called the Katy Flyer, that went from Kansas City to Dallas.

As these thoughts moved through my brain, I heard Granny Dickerson's voice from the kitchen.

"Charles, W.J. and Eva are here." I met W.J. as he got out of his car.

"Grandpa, what kind of car is that? It's beautiful."

"It's a Graham Page, Charles."

"Is it new, Grandpa?"

"Yep, just picked it up Saturday."

"Why didn't you bring Nelse, Grandpa?"

"Your Grandmother didn't want Nelson to miss school."

The trip to Bolivar in Grandpa's new Graham Page was a memorable one for me. Grandma Birt had engaged me in a conversation, wanting to know how my schooling was going, and if I was still singing in the Glee Club. What I did not tell her was that I had purchased steel traps with the money she had sent me as a bribe for singing in the Glee Club.

"Honey, Grandmother Dickerson told me that your teacher had sent a note to Ralph concerning voice lessons. What's that all about? Do you like singing?"

"It's OK."

When we arrived at the department store in Bolivar, I was impressed at the array of clothing the clerk was showing Grandmother and me. After some deliberation, I ended up with a pair of white slacks, white buck shoes, a white short sleeve shirt for dress, socks, underwear, and some everyday wash slacks, plus two summer shirts. I was ecstatic with all my new clothes, and Dad laughed and hugged me.

When we told Grandma and Grandpa goodbye, I told Granny to hug Nelse for me. She said she would and that I must come up this summer and visit Nelson.

"Charlie," Dad said while looking at my new clothes, "there won't be anyone at your graduation dressed as well as you are. Your Granny sure took care of you."

As I walked toward the high school, headed for graduation with my new duds on, I met two of the Aldrich locals who had guffawed and wanted to know where I was gonna preach.

One of my staunch friends, other than Marion Mitchell and Carl Hensley, was Paul Vincent. Paul and I spent many hours together fishing on Sac River at night. We liked to walk down the river until we found a bar of gravel on a riffle that extended into deep water. When we found a good riffle, we would make camp for the night, complete with a stack of firewood and a nice fire that produced a pot of boiling coffee. Sometimes we would fish until daylight, and we always had interesting conversations. Summertime in Aldrich presented a sort of Tom Sawyer-Huckleberry Finn existence for boys our age.

There were no jobs around Aldrich for teenage boys. In fact, there weren't any jobs for anybody of any age. The older men worked their gardens, mowed their lawns with a push lawnmower, and spent the afternoons playing checkers or croquet and discussing Franklin Roosevelt's New Deal, mostly in disparaging terms.

Paul and I, with lots of time on our hands and feeling

rather displaced in such an environment, often took to the river to seek solace in Mother Nature.

In the fall and winter, however, escaping the humdrum of Aldrich was not so difficult because we had school to command our attention, accompanied by basketball and, of course, trapping and hunting. I had about forty box traps for catching cottontails, which entailed a great deal of effort in getting the traps into a wooded area, baiting them, and setting them.

On Saturdays, Paul and I often spent the day searching hollow trees for possums. Since Paul was slightly crippled, I did all of the climbing. Paul would observe me as I climbed a tree that looked like a den tree. If the hole in the tree was too deep for me to determine whether or not the den contained a possum, I would poke a stick down in the hole. I could usually tell if the den contained the quarry we were looking for. Sometimes the den would yield a bevy of squirrels that would come out of the den like gangbusters. I would usually have my face close to the hole when the squirrels departed, and once or twice when this happened, I nearly fell out of the tree. Paul laughed.

One day, Paul and I ventured into the Stewart Woods to check on den trees. I had climbed a den tree and shouted to Paul that there was a possum in the tree but he was too far down in the den for me to reach him. Paul put some matches in his handkerchief, tied a rock to the handkerchief and threw it up to me. I lit one of the matches and threw it into the hole, knowing that all possums made their beds out of dried leaves. The tree den started smoking profusely, but the possum did not make his departure. In a very few minutes, I had a good fire going, so much so that I hastened to come down the tree. After a hurried consultation with Paul, we decided we should clear the area. We knew we could not put out the fire.

I was able to start up two or three pretty good fires in the big woods east of Aldrich that fall. The most disconcerting thing about these acts of arson on the sylvan landscape, which made Paul and me nervous, was we didn't get the possums. Somehow, they got away. We did do rather well at times, marketing the possums we found from 20 to 30 cents on the average.

One day, Paul and I were fishing for perch on the Coffman Branch. Suddenly, Paul said, "Charlie, let's start a Scout Troop." I was flabbergasted by his suggestion, but the longer he talked the more interested I became.

By the next day, we had notified, as I remember, ten boys between the ages of 12 and 14. Guys like Leonard Neil, Bernard Young, Murphy Perkins and Pete Curl responded to our directive to meet on the front steps of the Christian Church at 7 o'clock. When everyone seemed to be there, Paul furnished the following information.

We would meet once a week. We would camp out once every two weeks overnight. And we would have a series of athletic events so each Scout could improve his physical condition. The events would include boxing and wrestling and long hikes.

As I look back, I remember with great affection the guys who were in our troop during the summer of 1937. There was Pete Curl, who was a Navy pilot; Leonard Neil, who was a professor at Loyola University; Murphy Perkins, who was in executive sales most of his working life; and Bernard Young, who was an executive secretary.

Everyone in our Scout troop is no longer living. Paul

Vincent graduated from the University of Missouri with a degree in engineering and is also deceased. I graduated from Kansas State University and taught school for thirty years.

Paul, in spite of his crippled leg, was a very good baseball pitcher with a great curve ball. This fact become known when we played the Springfield Ike Martins on our very inferior field at the back of the Aldrich High School. We played very few games that summer, mostly because we had no transportation. When the Ike Martin team showed up to play us, they were not very complimentary on the condition of our field, which contained a quantity of pea-sized pebbles.

The Ike Martins, sponsored by a jewelry store in Springfield, displayed beautiful uniforms and leather gloves and spikes. When someone traveling with the team carried in a large sack of bats, we watched all of this display in silence. Bill Miller said, "Hell, boys. We only have two bats, and one of them is cracked. Maybe they will let us use some of their bats." Everybody laughed.

My envy at all the uniforms and bats probably showed, if anyone had been looking. My glove was one that Dad has used when he was a boy. I had cut out the pocket about the size of a baseball. When I caught the ball, it usually stung, but I didn't drop a single ball that I could get to.

To make a long story short, we beat the Ike Martins 6-5. I went one for four, but my one hit was a home run. I had never faced anyone who threw as hard as the Springfield pitcher. My dad sat with the father who told Dad his son had a contract with the St. Louis Cardinals.

The Ike Martin team came to Aldrich to play a practice game. They had no thought of losing. Even with all of their superior equipment, they couldn't beat us.

When I start to reminisce on the several pleasurable nights that, to the youth of Aldrich were like a Roman holiday, I would like to convey to the reader some idea of what transpired in the village of Aldrich on Halloween night.

First, a bunch of cronies would gather in Osa's Cafe a little bit after dark. Every citizen who observed this singular group realized the safety of their outdoor toilet would be in jeopardy. To counter this uncertainty, some people would go to great lengths to protect their toilets. There were several methods used to solve the problem, some of them rather comical. One method was to drive four posts into the ground around your facility and use barbed wire to tie the toilet down so it couldn't be moved. This situation did prove to be rather difficult to solve. Sometimes, if the toilet was too well secured, The Vandals, that was one of the names we went by, would move on to an easier target.

A few people would sit outside and guard their facilities, some even sporting a loaded gun. The main problem these people faced was their lack of patience. Sticking to their posts until about 2 a.m., some citizens would call it a night and retire. The attack on these people would be after the guard had retired for the night.

When our gang made an attack on a toilet, we expected to find a variety of safeguards in place. There was one safeguard we ran into that was far different than anything we had faced before. A particular citizen in Aldrich had quietly prepared a defense for his toilet by moving the toilet forward by about six feet. Dolan Crain led the ill-fated charge on this particular Halloween night. The rest of the gang was just far enough behind him to see Dolan go into the toilet pit almost up to his shoulders. Instead of administering the coup, we all stopped in time to laugh and laugh. Might it be said that Dolan left his fellow conspirators for the rest of the night, and the gentleman's toilet remained intact.

This little soliloquy would be incomplete without other remembrances of some of the personalities we had to deal with in carrying out our raids on Aldrich toilets.

There was the gentleman who cornered two of our gang in front of Stewart's Store. Even though Halloween was more than a week off, this gentleman described in detail what he would do if anyone attempted to turn his toilet over. He finished his oration by stating he would shoot the ass off anyone found on his property.

This threat presented an open invitation for some serious fun. Members of the gang decided they would post a watch so they could determine when the subject retired for the night. Then, they would turn his toilet. The guys watching the gentleman's house reported he had retired about 1 o'clock. So, the gang gathered out in the alley, ready to attack. As they were making ready for the rush, the gentleman walked off the back porch toward his toilet. It was almost 4 o'clock in the morning.

Dolan Crain said, "Let's turn it over with him in it."

Dote, as we sometimes called him, said he would slip up to the toilet and turn the door latch. And then he said, "When I say, 'charge,' you guys come up and help me push the toilet over." The next minute was very exciting. Dolan slipped up like an Indian and closed the door, turning the latch, and then he hollered, "Charge!" The toilet went over. I have never heard such cussing coming from inside a toilet. The gang departed rather rapidly for other parts. I don't know exactly what happened but was told neighbors came to the rescue.

I gave the gentleman in question a wide birth for six months. I think he knew who some of the culprits were, but as far as I know, he never harmed any of them.

I should mention that several members of the gang attended Ralph Taylor's Sunday school class. And, no, we did not bother little old ladies, nor cripples, nor people not able to right their toilets. We usually picked out people who would give us the best reaction.

Aldrich toilets were not the only target on Halloween. Some of the bigger boys, or should I say older boys, took a gentleman's new buggy apart and put it on the top of the Aldrich water tower and reassembled it. Such was Halloween night in Aldrich.

In the 1930s in Aldrich, youth did not have to be concerned with pedophiles or satanic cult members when they made the sojourn into a Halloween night. True, we didn't receive a sack full of candy for our efforts, but we were not subjected to candy with ground glass in it, or poison. I just recently noticed an article on Halloween that instructed parents whose children might go out trick-or-treating that known pedophiles would have to stay in designated areas previously set aside by the police. I think the article was referring to San Francisco. My, my. When a university professor said in class one day that change was constant, I thought of the change that had occurred in my lifetime. My grandmother took weeks to come from Kentucky to Missouri in a covered wagon, while my cousin Bernard flew from Kansas City to Los Angeles in a little more than two hours.

When I think back to my boyhood days in Aldrich during the Depression years, I remember some things very distinctly. I have to laugh when I think of tick tacking a matronly lady on a frosty Halloween night. Now the process that enabled us to tick tack was not mean or destructive. It required a simple length of string, some resin for the string, a tin can, and a nail. I will admit the clamor occurring from a tick tack presented strident noises that could be disruptive. For understandable reasons, I will not divulge the technique of the tick tack because I do not want the present generation to take on such trivialities.

The boys who had accompanied me, classmates all, knew the victim of our tick tacking would come unglued when she heard the noise, even if we didn't turn her outdoor toilet over. My small gang of conspirators also knew we would hear some choice words. There was no female in Aldrich who could call down curses on the heads of the guilty parties like this lady, unless it was the hellfire and damnation preacher who preached in one of the country churches in Polk County. I must advise that the hellfire preacher did not cuss at all but simply scared the hell out of us with his description of burning in an everlasting hell. The lady we were tick tacking seemed to know the entire lexicon of cuss words. One of my gang members asked me if I thought a person who cusses like that could go to heaven? I replied that I, too, wondered.

It is a fact that our enjoyment of the lady's blustery

outbursts resulted in extra visits to her home, without waiting for Halloween.

One summer morning Aldrich had some strange guests. Ike and Mike, a pair of doltish renegades, pulled their wagon into the alley alongside Poss Rotrock's Feed Store. Before these two gypsies had time to tie up their wagon, the word was out to hide everything that wasn't tied down because the gypsy people were very astute when it came to stealing. One Aldrichite, enjoying the diversion of this strange visit, warned the loafers perched on the cement sidewalk in front of Stewart's Store they had better look to their wives because gypsy men sure liked white women.

Meanwhile, Poss Rotrock had been approached by Mike, who was soliciting a little money or anything else Poss could offer so the two gypsies could get on their way to Illinois, where Mike's wife was in the hospital with pneumonia.

"What is your wife doing in Illinois?" Poss asked with a grin, though not expecting a straight answer.

Mike tugged at his heavy mustache and replied, "She went to visit her cousin." This remark prompted a chorus of loud guffaws.

Poss Rotrock, a nice man but unable to restrain himself, laughed pleasantly.

"Mike, I'll tell you what I can do for you. I have two cases of eggs that didn't pass the candle test. So here's what I will do, boys. I have a piece of canvass in the backroom that we can stretch across the alley on a rope. We will cut a hole in the canvass about the size of your head or just a little bigger. You can stand on a block of wood and stick your head through the hole and then let the boys throw eggs at your head. You will be down at the end of the alley, so you should be able to dodge any of the eggs that are thrown.

Mike looked around at the bunch of loafers who had edged up close enough to hear Poss's proposition. He didn't say anything but looked rather white.

Poss grinned and continued with his proposition. "Mike, I will sell the eggs two for a nickel, as long as the boys will buy them. You can have the entire proceeds. What do you think?"

Mike, getting whiter, finally agreed to the proposition, but he did not seem very resolute. Leastwise, the Aldrich loafers went gleefully about the task of putting the canvass in place and a wooden box for Mike to stand on.

The sale of eggs was brisk. Each man threw as straight as he could, but Mike, being very agile, was able to dodge even the best of throws.

As I watched the men throw their eggs, I was reminded of a carnival I had attended a while back, where men were throwing at a clown with his head also sticking through a hole in a canvass. They weren't able to hit him, either.

Perceiving some small discontent among the egg-throwing participants, I was not surprised to see two men throw at Mike simultaneously. Only by sheer luck was Mike able to dodge both throws. But the egg-throwers had noticed their comrades throwing more than one egg at a time. Someone said they saw four men throw eggs at one time. One egg struck Mike in the forehead and knocked him off the box. He must have lit running because some of the egg-throwers screamed like commanche Indians and took down the alley after him. I never saw Mike until later in the afternoon. Poss was trying to talk him out of calling the sheriff. Marion said they chased Mike until they got to the street where Mitch lived. Mitch said some of the guys were still throwing eggs.

Later on, I talked to a couple of the participants. They thought it was real fun, and as one man said, "It did liven up the town." This little escapade was the talk of the town for a week. Mike didn't call the sheriff and, according to Poss Rotrock, the pair departed town that same afternoon, with their egg money.

I had been after Mitch for some time to show me Uncle John's Civil War pistol. Finally, one morning we made a visit to Uncle John's house and found him sitting in his accustomed chair on the front porch.

"Hello, Grandpa," Mitch said matter-of-factly. "Charles wants to see your Civil War pistol."

Uncle John's smile was noticeable.

"It's in the kitchen in the top drawer of the cabinet."

With this statement, he met my gaze.

"How's Sara, Charles?"

"She's just fine, Uncle John," I said quickly. "She's still bothered by arthritis, though."

Uncle John laughed and remarked that he had the same problem.

"Poor people have poor ways, and richin's damn mean ones." Uncle John laughed, as if he was amused at what he said.

Later I told Dad what Uncle John had said, and Dad

also laughed.

"I suspect, Charlie, that Uncle John was sporting the populist view that rich people are mean, and poor people don't do well."

I did get to see Uncle John's revolver. It was a navy Colt and had to be loaded with powder and lead. When I asked Uncle John if he had ever shot at anyone with his revolver, he replied that he thought he had but couldn't remember for sure.

The gun was a great solace to me when Uncle John, on story nights, would give me permission to go to the cupboard and get his pistol to hold in my hand while he told me stories about the Civil War.

Years later, when I asked Marion what happened to Uncle John's revolver, Marion informed me that after Uncle John died, he kept the gun for a number of years but finally decided to give the gun to the museum in Bolivar, Missouri, where it is at present.

~～

One evening after supper Dad and I proceeded to Sara's porch swing. Dad was always in a storytelling mood when we occupied Granny's swing, and this night was no exception.

"Charlie, did I ever tell you about Spud Griffin?"

"No, Dad. You didn't. Who was Spud Griffin?"

"Spud Griffin was an old Civil War veteran who ran a restaurant here in Aldrich for several years in the '20s."

"What happened to him?"

"He died in 1924, I think."

"What about him, Dad?"

"Every evening Spud would blow Taps on his bugle.

People could almost set their watches by his bugle. He was famous for his chili. Everyone bragged on his chili. As time went by, his restaurant became a hangout for the young men of Aldrich. Since the 18th Amendment had become law, the young guys who patronized his place of business would drink their illegal whiskey in front of Spud. In fact, Spud would join the boys in a drink, which led to several fights and a budding reputation. Spud was a tough old geezer who tried to rein in the behavior of the young men but failed largely because, as he said, you need to raise a little hell now and then.

"The young men deviled Spud at almost every opportunity. They would throw live shells in his stove that heated the restaurant or stop up the stove pipe so everyone would have to clear the building. I remember one time they put Thompson, his cat, in the candy case. Whenever these events occurred, Spud would throw a tantrum, replete with classical cursing, and offer a $5 reward for telling him who was the culprit. I can't ever recall that he actually paid a reward. I always thought Spud enjoyed the tricks that were played on him. I know that when the boys left for World War I, Spud missed them, and when they returned in 1918, Spud became his old self, laughing or cursing, depending on the occasion, and offering his rewards for tricks the boys had played on him.

"When strangers to Spud entered his restaurant, they would, many times, be treated to Spud's customary soliloquy. 'Yep, I'm a Civil War veteran. Shot three times and hit in the head with a saber.' If the stranger evinced any interest, Spud would show them the huge scar over his left ear. If the customer still showed some interest, Spud would tell how he killed the 'Yellowbellie' that put the scar on his head. Spud was an interesting man,

Charlie. I really liked him."

"I would like to see a picture of Spud Griffin, Dad. Do you know of anyone around Aldrich who might have his picture?"

"No, Charlie. I don't. You were only 4 years old when he died. There weren't many cameras in Aldrich in those days."

I was beginning to get sleepy listening to Dad's story about Spud Griffin. A full October moon was just coming into view over the big hill. I had walked most of the day up and down Sac River fishing. My flagging interesting in Dad's story was revived when Dad made some remark about Spud almost being hung by some border ruffians when Spud was 16 years old.

"Charlie, Spud told me the story I'm going to tell you, when I was about 20 years of age, just before I married your mother. We were sitting in Spud's eatery. It was a cold winter day. Spud began his story by stating that he and his mother lived on a farm north of Aldrich, in the year 1862. One day, Spud said, three men rode up to their house. 'Ralph, I was in bed with the measles, but I knew something was wrong by viewing the three men out of my bedroom window. I saw them leading our two horses away from the barn. The men took two hams of meat hanging in the smokehouse and filled a sack with corn from our crib. They also took our one saddle.

"'I got up out of bed and proceeded to the front porch to see what was going on. One of the men was demanding money. Mother was crying, explaining that she only had $3, and was trying to talk the men out of taking our horses. One of the ruffians saw me standing on the porch and said, "Let's hang the kid." The ruffian then drug me out in the yard and took the rope from his saddle and put the rope around my neck. He threw one end of the rope over a limb of an oak tree that furnished shade for our yard. When he cinched the rope around my neck, Mother became hysterical. She dropped to her knees in front of one of the ruffians and sobbingly said, "Take everything we have, but don't hang my son." The three men laughed, gathered their loot and rode off. I was scared, Ralph, but I was also mad, very mad.'"

"Dad, what kind of people would do something like that? I don't understand. Were they Southern soldiers? Were they wearing a uniform?"

"No, Charlie. Men like that have always existed. The men stealing from Spud and his mother were ruffians, or bushwhackers. Call them what you will. They were not fighting for the North or South. They were just riding around the country robbing and pillaging and taking what they could from whomever. They were taking advantage of the fact that most of the men in any area were in the Army. They weren't afraid of women and old men."

"Did Spud know any of the three men?"

"He said he thought he had seen one of the men before. But, Charlie, there is more to this story. Spud said he was so mad he walked all the way to Springfield, with the measles, and enlisted in the Union Army."

"How far would that be, Dad?"

"Probably 35 miles."

Dad explained that Spud said he promised himself if he survived the war he would hunt those men down and kill them.

"'I never forgot what they did to my mother,' he said. 'When I came home from the war in May of 1865, Mother had been dead for about a month. She is buried in the Pleasant Ridge Cemetery in Aldrich.'"

Dad said, "I asked Spud if he located the three men after returning from the war."

"'Yes, Ralph. I found them,' he said. 'I killed all three of them, and I got away with it. It says in the Good Book, "Vengeance is mine sayeth the Lord." In my case, I hope the Lord is willing to forgive me for seeking my own vengeance.'"

As the people of earlier generations remember, the principal diet during the Depression years consisted of beans and corn bread, accompanied by baked sweet potatoes. The ingestion of beans and sweet potatoes combined almost always created a gaseous stomach condition that would last for some time.

Any pilgrim eating this sort of meal would, in polite company, need to control the noise that bean gas makes when it is expelled. Even manipulating the sphincter muscles around the anus in an attempt to lower the noise level by creating slide-outs is only about 30-percent effective. Besides the noise difficulty, there will be an odorous trail that will linger for some time after the initial expulsion.

When I broached the subject of farting with my father, he laughed and suggested that a change in diet might alleviate this problem but warned that a change of diet was not likely due to the increased cost, at least for most people. "Beans are the cheapest food to be had, and one of the best foods for you. Charlie, you remember what a doctor from Mayo Clinic said recently when asked about the single best food in the United States. He maintained that the best and most healthy food was beans. The poorest people are fortunate to have access to such a grand repast that is dirt cheap, don't you think? And easy to prepare."

I replied that I did think it was great that the poorest people had access to beans. I then asked him why my classmates at school were always passing gas, explaining that my teacher spanked one of my friends for not telling her what he was laughing at. He said he wouldn't tell her. But she threatened a spanking, so when he did tell her that George had let a fart, she spanked him, anyway, very hard.

"Charlie, in World War I, the Germans used poison gas made from different ingredients. Some of the boys that went to France told a group of us one day in Spud's restaurant after the war that some of the gas used contained a bean extract. I don't know if it is true, but that is what we heard from the boys."

I thought Dad's explanation was rather funny, but Dad was quick to tell me that my Uncle Willard, Dad's brother, was gassed during the war. Dad also remarked that 10,000 French soldiers were killed at the Battle of Verdun in about two hours. I think the Germans used phosgene gas in their attack."

"Did the phosgene gas contain a bean extract, Dad?"

"I don't think so."

"What makes beans so explosive, Dad?"

"I don't know exactly, but I know what a fellow in Kansas City told me after the war. The man said he mentioned in a conversation with one of his employees that he had been gassed during the Great War and that while in Germany he had heard that the Germans used an extract of beans for some of their poison gas. The man who was relating the story said his employee laughed and remarked that whoever said the Germans used bean extract to make poison gas didn't know what he was talking about, and besides that, there were no explosive qualities in the gas that came from navy beans. The employee was challenged by his employer to a test. The gent who was accepting the challenge was very adept at letting large farts and agreed to let his employer hold a lighted match to the gentleman's rear while he was in the act of passing gas.

The experiment was vastly successful. The employee passed his gas, grunted, and then screamed like a commanche Indian on the war path, charging forward like an NFL lineman running into a wall while cursing profusely. Dad laughed and said he often wondered about the extent of the man's injury. Later, Dad asked his friend who had applied the match what injuries the man sustained. His friend said there was no chance for a medical assessment because the man had taken off like a scalded cat and did not return to work until the next day. He never did divulge his injuries, if there were any, nor would he discuss the experiment.

After Clyde took over the feed store, he hired Tom Stevens to answer the phone, etc. Tom had fallen from grace when the Aldrich bank gave up the ghost in 1932, I think. Tom had worked as a teller.

As one could imagine, Tom enjoyed a great deal of leisure time working for Clyde. To help pass the time, being an ardent fisherman, Tom would bring his rod and reel to the feed store and practice casting in the street. He used a pretty good sized sinker for making his casts.

Someone, probably in fun, frayed his fishing line just above the sinker. So, one day when he was practicing casting, his sinker came off, hurtling into a large plate-glass window across the street in Stewart's Store, where it left a hole with small cracks radiating in every direction, much like a picture of the sunrise. Mr. Stevens was a fine Christian man, but I heard someone say that when Tom saw the sinker hit the large storefront window, he did some moderate cursing.

When Clyde Perkins was the depot agent in Deepwater, Missouri, he had been privy to a very comical event, and he picked a hot July afternoon to relate the story to me. There was no one in his feed store except him and me. The main street of Aldrich bore no visible signs of habitation. The one visible person was Osa Lowery, dozing in her restaurant across the street.

Clyde started by giving me a description of the man who was the centerpiece of his story. And even though the event that Clyde would reveal to me happened several years ago, Clyde had difficulty describing Lester Orford without laughing.

Lester was totally immersed in being a fireman. If you had a conversation with Lester, the subject matter would invariably turn to fire, or something related to fire, or how to put them out. Some people said that Lester was a firebug, partly because Lester sported a red fireman's hat and a silver whistle.

"Clyde, what is a firebug?"

"Charlie, a firebug could be a pyromaniac."

"Well, Clyde, what is a pyromaniac?"

"Charlie, a pyromaniac could be someone who is mentally unbalanced to the point that he has a compulsion to set things on fire."

"Was Lester a pyromaniac, Clyde?"

"I don't know, Charlie. I'll tell you what happened to Lester, and you can make up your own mind. I don't think he was, though."

Clyde continued by describing Lester as he appeared from day-to-day to the citizens of Deepwater.

"Lester was not a very big man, probably about 5 feet, 8 inches tall. He was known around town as a handyman. The only work I ever saw him do was mowing lawns."

"How old was he, Clyde?"

"I don't know, Charlie. I would guess him to be in his late 50s or early 60s."

"Where did he live in Deepwater?"

"He lived at the edge of town in a little house of maybe two rooms, just a shack. I don't think his house had ever been painted, at least not in this century," and Clyde laughed.

"Lester's attire was no less conspicuous than his behavior.

No one could say for certain where Lester had acquired his fireman's hat, until soon a Deepwater citizen claimed he saw the same hat in the Dime Store in Clinton. Previous to a citizen spotting what he claimed was the same identical hat that Lester was wearing, several people suggested the hat had been purloined from some fire station."

Clyde was laughing, "Most people debunked the idea of Lester stealing a fireman's hat because, as Charlie Hook said, Hook being the town barber, Lester had never left Deepwater, to his knowledge. And aside from that, I think Lester was honest. And Lester didn't have a car.

"Of course, everyone in town recognized Lester Orford. Most of the town loafers had spent hours discussing the fireman, and many wondered what the silver whistle was for. Lester was an enigma. While walking by the town loafers, who usually occupied the benches in front of the drug store, Lester would blow his whistle. His audience would cheer and shout to Lester, asking him where the fire was. Lester would look very dignified, in these instances, and would amble on down the street, and everybody would give him the horse laugh.

"One day, Lester walked into the mayor's office that was over Tilford's Grocery Store and requested to see the mayor. Now the mayor was a very nice man. He addressed Lester with a friendly howdy, thinking as he did so that some of the locals had not been very nice to Lester, and he had said so to some of the locals.

"Lester informed the mayor that he had invented a type of chemical that would extinguish fires.

"The mayor smiled. 'Congratulations, Lester. Are you going to seek a patent?'

"'No, mayor, my idea was to see if you could arrange to stack a bunch of flammable stuff out on the Main Street to set fire to. I could be up at my house so that you could call me on the phone and tell me that the fire is set. I would immediately move my wheelbarrow with a full barrel of my chemicals to the fire. You could time me, Mr. Mayor, and, if you are pleased, you might let me act as the Deepwater Fire Chief.'

"'Well, Lester,' the mayor smiled, 'that sounds like a good idea. How about Friday night? That's Halloween.

Could you be ready with your equipment by then?' A gleeful Lester assured the mayor he would be ready."

Friday morning dawned clear and cool. Drummers and other chance visitors were asking Deepwater citizens what all the trash was doing in the streets. The people that knew just laughed and kept on bringing all sorts of things to burn.

Clyde said that in the middle of town, junk was stacked as high as a one-story building. The people of Deepwater had made a prodigious effort to furnish fuel for Lester's fire.

"Finally, the time arrived for Lester to show his wares. He came down the hill pushing his wheelbarrow that carried a barrel of his concoction. He was moving remarkably fast, blowing his whistle and shouting for people to stand back. His haste had caused his fireman's hat to tilt to one side. People were shouting to him not to lose his hat. Not paying any mind to the crowd, he rolled the wheelbarrow close to a now prominent fire and squirted the liquid into the fire. Immediately, flames jumped sky high. Lester had to retreat."

"What happened, Clyde? Why did the flames get so high?"

Clyde was laughing again. "Some of the boys had gone up to his house yesterday while Lester was in town and poured out the chemical that he had in the barrel and replaced it with kerosene."

Clyde said he left Deepwater to come to Bolivar, but someone had told him that Lester had retired his firefighting equipment after his failed demonstration before the town. In fact, Lester never wore his fireman's hat again that anyone could remember."

"Is he still living, Clyde?"

"No, he died."
"Was he buried in Pottersfield?"
"Probably."

Junior Lyman, a friend of mine, related the following story to me concerning my great-grandfather who owned the hotel in Aldrich until it burned down in 1929.

It seems that a minister of one of the churches in Polk County came in on the evening Frisco train from Kansas City. Since the train was very late and Aldrich was being buffeted by snow and heavy winds, the minister went to the Perkins Hotel to get a room for the night.

John Perkins met him at the door of the hotel and greeted him, for he and the minister were good friends. When the minister announced he wanted a room for the night, Uncle John told him that it was 9 o'clock and all of his guests were asleep and that the reverend would have to be careful not to awaken anyone. The minister said he would be quiet. So Uncle John told him to proceed to the second room on the right upstairs and not to turn on any lights but to undress and get in bed as quietly as he could. Uncle John told him good night, and the minister proceeded up the stairs to his appointed room.

It wasn't long until Uncle John heard a curdling scream. A woman in mid-life made her disheveled appearance on the stairs, her night cap was partly obscuring her face, and the gown that she was wearing was too small for such a buxom woman. She was shouting something very loud, possibly some expletives. Uncle John asked her what was wrong, and she said something about a man trying to attack her. Uncle John Perkins was unperturbed. He apologized and tried to explain that he sent the minister of God up to the wrong room, and he told the lady to go back to her room and he would straighten everything out. By this time, the minister of God had made his appearance. He was very docile, but listened to Uncle John's explanation and quickly went back up the stairs to his new room. The lady, an old maid school teacher, informed Uncle John she would never again take a room in his hotel. My great-grandfather later laughed about the incident when he told hotel occupants the next morning what had happened. Junior Lyman said John Perkins just wanted to liven up the place.

Part Two

The day shall not be up so soon
As I, to try the fair adventure
Of tomorrow.
—Shakespeare

While growing up in Aldrich, I was pretty much unaware of the black race. There were no negroes in Aldrich and only one black family in Bolivar, twelve miles away. True, there were several negroes in Springfield, but Springfield was forty five miles away.

From time to time I would hear Rochester, Jack Benny's negro butler, talking to Jack Benny on our Atwater Kent radio, and remembered the negro dancer who came through Aldrich with a traveling medicine show. Other than that, I had little opportunity to see a black person. As time went by, I found myself slowly stereotyping the negro, with the scant knowledge I had gathered from acquaintances. When I read Mark Twain's *Tom Sawyer* and Dad told me about the three negroes who were lynched on the square in Springfield in 1901, the year Dad was born, my curiosity was expanded.

One day when returning from school I saw my father,

along with several other men, digging a ditch along the road. I was really surprised to find my father digging a ditch on the front street of Aldrich and stopped to ask him what he was doing. His reply was that he was paying his poll tax. When I began to question him further, he told me to go on home, that he would explain the poll tax to me later. When I questioned Dad that evening concerning the poll tax, he informed me he could either pay his poll tax with cash, which he didn't have, or he could work it out, and that's what he was doing.

"Dad, do negroes have to pay poll taxes?"

"No, Charles."

"Why not?"

"Negroes can't vote."

"Could you vote, Dad, if you didn't pay your poll tax?"

"No, I couldn't, Charlie. Everyone has to pay a poll tax. That's the reason negroes can't vote. They don't have the money to pay their poll tax. At least it is one of the reasons."

"Well, Dad. Can the negroes who have enough money to pay their poll tax vote?"

"No, Charles. They can't."

"Why not, Dad? The negroes live in this country. I don't see why they can't vote."

"Charles, a decision by the United States Supreme Court in the last century ruled that the negro was not a person. The 14th Amendment says that no state shall deny to any person the equal protection of the law. If the negro is not a person under the court's ruling, then the state can deny equal protection to the negro."

"Dad, if the negro isn't a person, what is he?"

"Well, Charlie, the infamous Dred Scott decision of

the last century has gone by the boards. White society has done everything it can to keep the negro from voting in this century. For example, the South has used literacy tests, tests on the U.S. Constitution, to qualify negroes for voting. There is the poll tax, which I've explained to you. But one of the most pernicious things that the white man has done to the negro is a myriad of threats against the negro if he chooses to vote — loss of his job or the threat of bodily harm to himself and his family, including burning his house down. With all of the running threats to the Southern negro, the South has become known as the Solid South, meaning that most people in the Southern states vote the straight Republican ticket."

"Dad, I'm sure glad I'm not a negro. I feel sorry for them."

"I do, too, Charlie, but that's pretty much the way things are, especially in the South. If you are a negro who desires to vote, you must register. Registration itself will make you a marked man because the white man knows you are planning on voting. You can imagine the various economic forces imposed on the negro by a white society who knows everything."

"Dad, how do you know all of these things? How did you know about the Dred Scott decision or the 14th Amendment?"

"I read books, Charlie. I read books. Why do you think I bring books to you from the school library? To read. To read. If you don't read, you actually have no advantage over those who can't read."

I searched my father's countenance, noting his earnestness. I remembered the several students from Aldrich High School who had come by the house to consult Dad on difficult algebra problems.

One day Dad and I had a conversation that led to me disclosing what I had seen the previous morning on the way to school.

"Dad, I saw two negroes yesterday morning on the southbound Frisco freight train heading for Springfield."

Dad smiled. "They were hoboes."

"Is that what you call them? They were riding in an open box car, and they were grinning and waving. I waved back."

"Remember, Charles, those young black men you saw have no rights as citizens. They are probably heading for Springfield to find some sort of employment. Negroes can't find much in the way of employment in the small towns. They need to live in large cities where the menial jobs are."

"Dad, what is a menial job?"

"Charlie, menial jobs are the jobs that don't require any education or training. That's the reason most negroes in the South are employed as sharecroppers in the rural areas. In this manner, they can pretty much dodge the Jim Crow Laws."

"What are Jim Crow Laws, Dad? I don't think you have mentioned Jim Crow Laws before."

"Charlie, they are laws that restrain the negro in several respects. Jim Crow Laws separate the races. Negroes can't eat in white men's restaurants, nor can they receive a haircut in a white man's barber shop. If they want to attend a movie, they must find a movie house with a balcony so they can be seated or segregated away from the white man. And last, but not least, the negro can't use white men's toilets or drinking fountains."

"Dad, I didn't know all of these things about the negro. Why are they treated so badly?"

"Well, Charlie, they only comprise about nine to ten percent of the population. They are a minority. Generally, minorities are not treated too well in any society. There are other reasons which you will discover for yourself as you go through life. You could, in some ways, compare the persecution of the negroes with that of the Jews.

"You mentioned the other day that you were beginning to stereotype the negro in your own mind. After our conversation on the black race, Charlie, what is your opinion of the negro as you have listened to my conversations? Is your position more positive? I realize that your opinion on the negro race must be made without much direct observation. You must have formed some sort of opinion, though, and your opinion today should carry a more positive note, or a more negative note, than when we started delving into the negro race. Your enlightenment would naturally bring change to your previous sentiment on this subject."

"Dad, you have really told me a lot concerning the negro. I feel that I know a lot more than I did when we began these conversations. But Dad, I don't really know how to answer your questions concerning my impression of the negro. I can say I felt awfully sorry for the negro and wish I could change some of the things that seem to me to be so wrong. The Jim Crow Laws are where I would start to insist on change."

"Charlie, for a 12 year old, I'm so glad to see you interested in the affairs of the world. As you mature, your whole philosophy of life will change to some extent. But the key is to keep on reading, to keep on studying, to read current newspapers and magazines, and study the English language."

"I will, Dad. I will."

"And, Charlie, the study of Jewish people is also very, very interesting. They have been persecuted from one end of the world to the other end. As you may know, the Jews have suffered terribly from the charge that they crucified Christ. Beyond that, Henry Ford, the car manufacturer, charged a Jew with being the author of a white paper, called the 'Protocols of Zion,' that contained a plan for the Jews to dominate the world economically."

"Wow, Dad. You think the high school library would have any information on the Jews?"

"I'm sure it would. If not, you can read the Bible."

When I remember conversations with my dad over all those years, I think how lucky I was to have had such a father. True, he was a bootlegger, but he was a very interesting father. As I think back, I could never have foreseen a "black caucus" in the American Congress.

≈≈≈

The story of the snowbound train has always fascinated me. Here is the story as Dad related it to me many years later.

"In the first week of January in 1918, I boarded the morning Frisco passenger train in Aldrich, bound for Knasas City. I was headed for Morris, Kansas, a small town to the south of Kansas City, to take my first permanent job as station agent and telegrapher on the Frisco Railroad."

"How old were you, Dad?"

"I was sixteen years old, and I had never been away from home any length of time before my trip to Morris, Kansas, on that January morning."

As Dad recounted, the train had a goodly number

of passengers aboard, and it was beginning to snow as the train pulled out from the Aldrich station. He also noticed a particular chill in the air, which reminded him of the overcoat he was wearing, because of his mother's insistence.

"Ralph," Sara had said with some finality, "take your overcoat." Before the day was over, Ralph Dickerson would be very thankful for his mother's guidance.

The railroad coaches, even in 1918, Dad had explained, were comfortable enough. They were heated by warm steam from the engine pulling the train.

As the train progressed north toward Kansas City on that wintry morning, the snow became very heavy, blotting out much of the landscape. Dad said he was enjoying the snowfall, so pretty across the countryside, but did notice the visibility out his coach window was becoming more limited. This snow was really heavy, perhaps the biggest snow storm Dad had ever witnessed in all of his sixteen years.

Dad ordered a cup of coffee and a doughnut from the porter who had made frequent trips through each coach, selling his wares from a wicker basket.

Charlie Morrison, the conductor, aware that Dad was traveling on a Fricso pass, had inquired of Dad's status, and was very complimentary when he learned that Dad was a telegrapher. Morrison had been with the Frisco for thirty-five years and advised Dad that the snow was about as deep in the cuts as any storm he had experienced. Dad laughingly asked Mr. Morrison what the chances were that the train would falter in the deep snow. Charlie had replied that if the snow stopped this train, it would be a first.

By lunchtime, the porter was busy serving hot coffee

and sandwiches, along with the fruit and candy. He had told Dad the snowstorm was good for business, stating he didn't have a thing left except a few packages of gum.

After finishing his lunch, Dad made his way to the smoker at the far end of his coach to have a cigarette, momentarily forgetting the outside weather. The smoker was already occupied by three men who were engaged in a discussion on whether or not the United States should join the League of Nations. Cigar smoke permeated the smoking car until Dad opened a window. The three gentlemen did not hesitate with their discussion, the noisiest gentleman proclaiming that we should continue with our policy of isolationism. Dad surmised that the three gentlemen were drummers, on their way to wherever to peddle their wares. They seemed to be so immersed in their discussion that Dad wondered if any of the three were cognizant of the huge storm outside the train.

Dad returned to his seat and was having an interesting conversation with a woman across the aisle.

It was about 4 o'clock in the afternoon when it became apparent to Dad that the train was struggling in the deep snow. He could tell the train's speed was considerably diminished. The landscape, through the frosted windows, was moving very slowly. Several times, the big steamer almost came to a dead stop. Finally, after backing up twice, the engine again started forward. Then the train stopped for good. My father's woman companion inquired as to what town they had entered. Dad replied that he didn't think they were in a town, but rather, they were stuck. The lady laughed.

Dad said he walked to the end of his coach and opened the door leading into the vestibule. The door to the vestibule, where passengers normally departed the train, was frozen shut. To Dad's amazement, as he peeked through a spot on the window, which he had cleaned off, snow was packed up to the window ledges on the outside of the train. From what Dad could make out, the train was settled in a deep cut. Snow was coming down so rapidly it was an absolute blizzard, with almost no visibility.

The realization struck Dad that the coaches would cool off rather rapidly without the steam heat. As he approached his seat, he was aware of the young woman occupying the seat in front of him. She was accompanied by a small child, and neither the child nor its mother seemed to be adequately dressed for the occasion.

Dad gave the woman his overcoat, and she smiled and murmured a low, "Thank you."

Already, there was a chill in the air. Dad said he was thankful his mother had insisted he take his overcoat. As he walked up and down the aisle to keep warm, here came the conductor, Charlie Morrison, making his way through the coaches, being bombarded with questions.

One fellow began to chant, "Turn up the heat."

Morrison would laugh and repeat his position by saying, "Yes, we are stuck in a snow drift, but don't worry. We will get out of it."

The brakeman came along behind the conductor, checking on the passengers and apologizing for the train's lack of heat. He gave the cold passengers some hope when he announced he was going to try to make it to a farm house that he knew of a little more than a mile from the stalled train. One passenger wanted to know what he would do if he found the farm house.

The brakeman replied, "I'll call the head dispatch in Kansas City and have him send an engine to pull us out."

"God, I hope you make it," one passenger exclaimed.

Another female passenger asked if the snow wasn't awfully deep.

"Yes, mam, it is. But I can make it," replied the brakeman as he made his way into the next coach.

Dad continued walking the length of the coach, trying to keep warm. It was getting steadily colder. He said he felt sorry for the women and children and could tell they were having a hard time keeping warm. The woman Dad had given the overcoat to had wrapped his overcoat around herself and the child.

By now it was pitch black outside, and the windows of the coach were coated with frost. The wind howled out of the north.

About 10 o'clock Dad walked up to the end of the coach to see if he could see anything. He had been trying to sleep, but the cold wouldn't permit him to. Walking the length of the coach and back helped a little. As he opened the coach door into the vestibule he felt a rush of cold air. Rubbing a spot on the vestibule door with his fingers, he was able to see the snow had stopped. The moon was shining brightly on a winter wonderland. The weather had cleared, but the cold was brutal.

Dad said he was about half asleep in his seat when he felt the lurch of the steamer as it attached itself to the stalled train. People who were dozing stood suddenly and yelled out. It was about 4 o'clock in the morning, but everyone in Dad's coach, as cold as they were, made little peek holes on the frosted windows so they could see the train moving in the winter night. The steamer pulled Dad's train to Raymore, Missouri, where the half-frozen passengers were treated to bacon, ham and eggs, and hot biscuits at the hotel. There was also lots of hot coffee. Dad said he could never remember a breakfast that tasted as good as the one he had that cold morning in Raymore, Missouri.

⁓

On November 7, 1908, Henry Starr and a companion arrived in Fair Play, Missouri, on the morning train. When the two gentlemen stepped down on the cinder platform, they took in the Main Street of Fair Play in one glance. Their demeanor was guarded. They had come to rob the Fair Play bank.

Noticing a crowd of people south of the train depot, Henry Starr stopped a passerby and inquired as to what the people were doing. The man explained that Bill Akard was putting on a shooting exhibition and he had just returned from Russia, where he put on a shooting exhibition for Czar Nicholas II. Henry was notably impressed and said so. Encouraged by Henry's attitude, the Fair Play citizen revealed that Bill Akard had also put on a shooting exhibition for the King of England and that Mr. Akard was the best damn shot in the world. Henry Starr and his companion were impressed, especially so when they watched Mr. Akard bust two glass marbles by firing over his left shoulder while looking into a mirror to see the target.

Henry Starr, an excellent pistol shot, was heard to remark that he didn't want Bill Akard shooting at him.

After a hurried consultation, the two conspirators caught the afternoon train for Aldrich, Missouri, six miles to the south. They would rob the Aldrich bank in the afternoon, and my dad would be there.

My father, Ralph McKinley Dickerson, died in his 96th year in 1997. For several years, I had often appealed to Dad to let me tape some of the stories and experiences he had encountered in his long life. I would sometimes remark to Dad that he owed something to his progeny, and perhaps, to posterity. He would laugh and then embark on another funny story.

Dad finally complied to my requests to tape his stories. We spent many winter evenings laughing and remembering. R.D., as I often called him, was a super storyteller with a great memory. But he was no clown. He was very bright.

The tapes that he and I made were kept in my desk drawer for almost five years after his death.

Ralph M. Dickerson was born in 1901, while William McKinley was president. Sara Dickerson, Ralph's mother, and an ardent Republican, who would have refused to vote for her own brother if he had been a Democrat, gave my father his middle name of McKinley.

Dad told me on one occasion that he could remember his father discussing the Russo-Japanese war with a neighbor in 1905. But his best early remembrance was when the Aldrich bank was robbed in 1908 by two outlaws, one of which was Henry Starr, the infamous bank robber.

Dad remembered it was November and he was in the second grade.

"I was coming down the alley by the blacksmith shop," Dad said, "when I noticed Zelma Toalson and another man walking side-by-side toward the west.

The stranger had a gun in his hand. When I made my appearance at the end of the alley, the stranger looked at me and kept walking, Zelma Toalson at his side. All of a sudden, Zelma and the stranger stopped, about where the farmer's exchange is. Zelma turned around and started back toward the bank, while the stranger with the big gun continued walking west. A man in a buckboard pulled by two horses picked up the stranger and headed down the Sac River road on the dead run."

"Dad, who was the stranger? Was he Henry Starr?"

"Yes, Charlie, the man escorting Zelma down the road was Henry Starr.

"By this time, Charlie, several people were aware the bank had been robbed. The sheriff, or rather the deputy and only lawman in Aldrich, was around on the north side of town at the produce house, where my brother Bert was busy picking turkeys.

"A breathless Aldrich citizen had run up to the deputy and informed him that the bank had been robbed and the robbers were headed down the river road in a buckboard that was going like a bat out of hell.

"The deputy, visibly shaken by the news, asked the group of men present if anyone would ride with him to go after the outlaws. When no one volunteered, Bert said he would go, but he didn't have a horse. Someone told Bert to take his horse, and he and the deputy took off in a gallup.

"Charlie, Bert was only 17 years old, but he wasn't afraid of anything. Bert told me that he and the deputy rode their horses on the dead run to the Sac River bridge. When they got to the bridge, Bert said the deputy reined in his horse and informed Bert that he had forgotten his gun. Dad said Bert had laughed and remarked that the deputy didn't really want to chase the outlaws. After that event, the deputy was asked several times if he had his gun with him. His gun had become a standing joke.

"In the meantime, one of the Aldrich citizens had a brainstorm. He called the Lyman residence, which was situated about thirty feet from the river road. Dad said he told the Lymans that they should try to stop the robbers, who would be coming by their house in just a few moments, that the bank would probably pay a reward for their capture. It so happened that the Lymans were preparing to go quail hunting when they received the phone call. In their own words, the two Lyman boys hid in a ditch by the side of the road that contained a sizeable plum thicket, armed with loaded shotguns. The Lyman boys said they didn't have long to wait. The buckboard was coming toward the Lymans at a rapid rate. One of the Lyman boys said Henry Starr was sitting on the left side of the buckboard and that he had a six-shooter in each hand.

"The Lyman boys said, 'Hell, we let 'em go.'

"Bert said the Lymans could have killed both of the robbers if they had had the nerve, since the buckboard passed within twenty-five feet of where the Lyman boys were hidden in a plum thicket.

Legend has it that Henry Starr, Bell Starr's nephew by marriage, was sentenced to death in 1895 by Judge Parker. The sentence was reversed by the State Supreme Court in the same year.

Witnesses to Henry's trial said that Henry called Judge Parker "Old Nero" and bullied the judge by telling him he had faced down tougher people than the judge. These words made Judge Parker mad, so he gave Henry the death sentence. It didn't stick.

Henry Starr was killed while robbing a bank in Oklahoma. Henry had put the president of the bank in the vault, thinking that he had locked the vault. When he noticed a little boy crying in the front of the bank, Henry asked the little guy what was wrong. The little boy was worried about his dad in the vault. Henry consoled him, gave him some new pennies, and started to leave the bank. The banker shot him from the vault.

As Henry Starr lay dying, he swore that he had never killed a man.

Poss Rotrock had his feed store in the building known as the Red Onion, directly across the street from Stewart's Hardware Store. There was an upstairs to the Red Onion that ran the length of the building with a small stage at the north end. The second floor had a wide assortment of benches and chairs, which were used whenever a movie was shown. The entrance to the second floor was reached by outside stairs on the west side of the building that led to the one entrance to the upstairs theater. This arrangement made it impossible for me to slip into the movie when I didn't have the 10 cents for admission. Marion Mitchell always got in free to the movies because his mother owned the Red Onion.

When the circus came to town once a year, they pitched their big tent on the Frisco right-of-way. Mitch and I were always able to crawl under the tent and get in free. But if I wanted to see the weekly movie in the Red Onion, I had to have the cash, for the guy running the projector stood right by the door during the movie.

Mitch and I looked forward each week to the

serial shown, following the movie, which featured Jack Armstrong, the all-American boy. Jack Armstrong ended the last few scenes each week attempting to keep from getting killed by alligators, sharks or villains of one kind or another. From week to week, the Armstrong serial generated lots of discussion from participants who liked to speculate on how Mr. Armstrong would save himself. But Jack Armstrong continued to live and thrive, and the Aldrich citizens kept coming when they could raise 10 cents.

I attended the last weekly movie in the Red Onion. It was a cowboy movie, followed by the Armstrong serial. Unfortunately, Jack Armstrong was killed. This made the moviegoers in Aldrich very mad, and they went home declaring their hero was dead. It was the talk of the town.

When the man who showed the movies came to Aldrich on Tuesday night next, he found only three people in the theater. When he asked what was wrong, one of the three ticket-paying citizens informed him that Jack Armstrong was dead and the people would not grace the Aldrich theater again. The gentleman explained that Jack Armstrong was not really dead, but the serial ended with a new contract for Jack Armstrong, who would now be working for another studio. As far as they were concerned, Jack Armstrong was dead because they saw him fall off the cliff and into a stream that was full of alligators.

The Red Onion withstood another minor depreciation when Poss Rotrock grew tired of pleading with certain Aldrich citizens not to urinate in his coal bin in the alley back of the feed store. In the summer, the smell would become rather intense. To correct the situation, Poss made what he called the "pee plate." This metal plate that Poss had concocted was electrically charged. The pee plate was laid on the ground in the coal bin and was covered over with a tad of dirt for purposes of concealment. I knew that a charged metal plate would induce quite a reaction because I had watched Ching Stevens and Barney Toalson construct a plate covered with grains of corn. Barney brought a Rhode Island red rooster in the workshop and set the rooster down by the side of the plate. The rooster took one look and pecked away for a kernel of corn. The rooster jumped at least five feet high and squawked loudly and decided he would pass the corn.

The first victim of the pee plate, according to witnesses, screamed and roared out into the alley, falling down and clutching his groin. The word was quickly passed that you should not pee in Poss Rotrock's coal bin.

When Poss Rotrock moved from Aldrich, my cousin Clyde Perkins, another victim of the railroad seniority system and a telegrapher like my father, took over the Red Onion feed store. Clyde, a very amiable man and a great storyteller, made the feed store a regular hangout. Ching Stevens would bring his guitar to the feed store, where he and I would sing and sing.

Spugh Meyers, resident pharmacist in Aldrich, was so captivated by our singing that he announced he would buy our bus ticket and our meals if we would go to Springfield and audition at KWTO radio station. "Boys," he said, "you guys are better than anybody on the radio in Springfield." I would have taken the offer, but Ching said we were not as good as Spugh thought we were. So we just continued our singing in the Red Onion and at school functions. When we received a crowd response for an encore, Ching would say, "I will only answer one encore."

Granny Dickerson was a good Christian woman in my eyes, and I always listened carefully to what she said concerning religion and the Bible. One saying I remember her for was "lips that touch whiskey will never touch mine." "That's what I told your grandfather, Charles, and he quit drinking completely." When I heard Granny make this pronouncement, I wondered if she included wine in her denouncement of spirits. I don't recall asking her, but I wanted to tell her that somewhere in the Bible it stated that a little wine was good for the stomach. This utterance from the Bible was sometimes used to reprove my Baptist friends who were opposed to drinking anything of an alcoholic nature.

Sara, or Granny, as I usually called her, had several curative medicines in her cupboard, some of which I abhorred. I was always induced by Sara, in the spring of the year, to take sulfur and molasses, perched on a cracker. Sara called this medication my spring tonic. She maintained that sulfur and molasses would purge my blood.

And then there was castor oil, which almost made me puke, and, finally, the skunk oil that Granny applied to my chest when she thought I had a chest congestion. That stuff had an awful smell, as you can imagine. These remedies seemed about as worthless to me as the goat glands that Dr. John R. Brinkley of Delrio, Texas, talked about on our Atwater Kent radio late at night.

The only concoction I really enjoyed was the sassafras tea that Granny made. I would go out along the roadside on gravel roads in the summer and harvest the sassafras tree roots. Granny would deposit the barks and tree roots in a closed fruit jar. When winter came, we would have sassafras tea and homemade cookies. Granny would laugh and tell me that sassafras tea was good for the blood.

Now you may be fostering the idea that Granny was some sort of medical quack because of all the home remedies she prescribed. Some so-called moderns likened people like Granny to the Medicine Man in an Indian tribe. But I am here to tell you that for the seven years I spent with Sara, she cured every cold and fever and treated my numerous chigger bites by having me bathe in the branch, or the duckhole, using her homemade lye soap. She doctored my measles, chicken pox, and whooping cough. Some of the remedies she used died with her. I have heard from my father the story of her catching the train in Aldrich to travel to Stanley, Kan., where her 16-year-old son (my father) lay dying from the Spanish flu. She cured him almost immediately. She probably used many of the home remedies her ancestors brought from Ireland. Twenty million people died from Spanish flu.

The only time Granny was so confused she called Dr. Meyers was when I told my father, on a beautiful spring morning, that I had no symptom of sore jaws and proceeded to walk down Sac River, wading and having a great time fishing for bass.

The following morning, after our fishing trip, it was obvious that something was wrong. My testicles had begun to swell, so Granny called the doctor. In those days, doctors made house calls.

After examining me, Doc Meyers explained to Sara that I had the mumps and they had "gone down" on me and that I would have to lie flat on my back, with one leg in a sling — up high — for a few days until the swelling went down. This was a horrible sentence for an active boy like me.

Shell Toalson lived across the street from the Mitchell residence. I used to borrow books from the Toalson's library. Kathleen Toalson, Shell's youngest daughter, would let me borrow two books at one time, which was great. Shell Toalson had been my Sunday School teacher at the old Christian Church when I was around 10 years of age.

One day after school, my father was sent by his mother to get a gallon of milk from Mrs. Shell Toalson. As he approached the Toalson residence, Shell's pointer bird dog ran out of the back yard into the street and started biting him. Dad said he threw up his arms to protect his face, sustaining several bites on his arms.

A man whose name Dad couldn't remember ran the dog off and took Dad home, where Sara doctored his bites.

When Robert Dickerson, my grandfather, returned home from his job at the mill, he listened as Sara explained what had happened to Dad. Rather angry at what had occurred, Robert took his 12-gauge shotgun out and loaded it. He walked calmly down the hill to the Toalson residence, where Shell was standing on the front porch.

"Shell, I've come to kill your dog."

Dad said that Shell replied, "Go ahead, Robert. He's out there in his pen."

So Robert Dickerson and Shell Toalson, who were the best of friends, were saddened by the loss of a state champion class pointer.

Speaking of school spankings, my father has told me of the spanking he received when he was 10 years old. Dad could recall the event because it was inextricably tied to the Aldrich Bank robbery by Henry Starr in 1908. Dad was using Henry Starr's robbery of the Aldrich Bank to help him remember the worst spanking he ever received.

"Charlie, I was 10 years old when this redheaded teacher spanked me."

"Dad, from what Granny tells me, the word spanking is a misnomer. What the redheaded teacher gave you was a beating. I think Granny would have beat the hell out of her, if she hadn't left town."

Dad laughed and said, "Charlie, she was about six feet tall and sorta ugly. The day she whipped me, another student threw me a ball, which I caught. This little episode occurred after the bell had rung for class to take up. The teacher walked back to my seat and said, 'Ralph, you stay in after school.' I didn't say anything, but I made up my mind that she wasn't going to whip me unless she whipped the boy who had thrown me the ball. Well, when school was out, I started out the door, but she restrained me, stating she was gonna whip me. I told her I would take a whipping if she would also whip the boy who had thrown the ball to me. She didn't answer my charge but took a switch out of the closet and started to swing it at me. Charlie, a hickory switch really hurts, but I didn't cry, and I didn't beg. She kept shouting for me to cry, but I refused. Charlie, she literally beat the blood out of my back. By the time I got home, my shirt was stuck to my back. Mother was boiling mad. She soaked my back with hot towels, removed the shirt and doctored my back with some kind of salve."

My grandfather, home from the mill where he worked as a millwright, was advised by Granny as to what had happened. Granny, through doctoring me, picked up a horse whip from our back porch and started out the door. Robert said, "Sara, now don't do what you are about to do. Let it go." According to Dad, Mother said, "Robert, get out of my way. I'm going to find that woman, and when I do I'm gonna whip her." Well, the story ended peacefully. The lady teacher left town for the weekend. Sometime later, Sara had a conversation with the teacher at school. "Don't ever whip my son again."

Mitch and I often discussed the topic of salvation and what one had to do to achieve it. Since we both attended different Sunday schools, we always were able to consider two different approaches.

I remember that in the late '30s Adolph Hitler was the Biblical Antichrist, depending on which set of Aldrichites you were listening to. The other candidate for such a hideous part was Joseph Stalin. As I look back, I think that both groups must have been wrong, since neither one of these gentlemen are living at the present time. If you had awarded that man who was able to kill the most people, Joseph Stalin would have won.

To say I spent the young years of my life in the Bible Belt of Missouri would be true. In fact, I am glad I was surrounded and, in many cases mesmerized, by the conflicting ideas that came from people who had read the Bible through, and in many cases, several times. My answers to questions that I had put to these good people were laced with what people today would call fundamentalism. When I asked my father what was good or bad about fundamentalism, my father replied that the people who took a fundamentalist viewpoint were the people who weren't looking for the easy road to heaven. I don't agree with some of the things that fundamentalists believe, but they do take the hard road.

When grandmother told me her belief regarding rich men going to heaven because that's what it said in the Bible, I felt bad.

"It is easier for a camel to go through the eye of a needle than it is for a rich man to go to heaven," Grandmother had told me in complete earnestness.

Years later, in a conversation with a university professor who had achieved a doctorate from the Yale Divinity School, the professor had labeled my grandmother's interpretation as absurd. His explanation was that the burning dump outside the gates of Jerusalem was the real hell. People who wrote the Bible wanted to create the worst hell they could envision in those days, if one did not follow God's teaching. Hence, the burning lake of fire. He then said the needle was, in reality, an archway leading out of the Holy City. When a camel went through the needle, the camel had to stoop down to get through the needle. Thus, the Biblical verse about the camel going through the needle was symbolism. A rich man had to be humble and stoop to find the kingdom of heaven. In direct contrast to what Grandmother had told me, rich men could go to heaven if they humbled themselves, he said.

"I cannot find the word rapture in the Bible," a minister had told me in all confidence. "However, I do not say that the Bible's explanation of God taking all of his people to heaven in one felled swoop to protect them from the horrible last days is the rapture that people in the different churches believe in. I simply do not know, Charles."

My education in music was rather sparse but extended through the High School Glee Club, a couple of operettas and the junior play, where I enjoyed a short romance with one of the Davis girls. I did not take part in the senior play due to scheduling difficulties and my relationship with the Cauble sister, my newest amour.

However, I must disclose that the music teacher sent me home with a note declaring that my talent as a singer was unquestionable and I needed voice lessons. My father, upon receiving this communiqué, sent a note of inquiry back to the teacher wanting to know how much individual voice lessons would cost. When I presented Father with the answer to his inquiry (It was on a Friday.), I had a hollow feeling in my stomach. The voice lessons would cost 50 cents per lesson. I was immediately reminded of the conversation Dad had with the dentist in Morrisville the previous week, when Dad had informed the dentist that my two fillings would have to wait. The fillings were to cost 50 cents per tooth.

"Charlie, our present condition is lamentable, but things will change. This Depression will have to end sooner or later. I'm sorry I can't afford your voice lessons. Maybe later."

"That's all right, Dad. I think I'll go over to Vina's house and listen to her Victrola."

Vina had invited me to come over and listen to her records several times, but I had always declined for one reason or another.

As I made my way to Vina's front door, I realized I would have to go another route if I wanted to be a singer. Vina greeted me with a smile and said to come in. She took me into her front room and offered me a chair. All of her furniture was, as Dad had described it, Victorian. I looked at Vina. Her kind face bore a slight smile. I wondered how old she was. It seemed that Granny Dickerson mentioned 90-something.

"Charles, do you want me to play the Victrola for you?"

"Yes, Vina, I would like to hear one of your Caruso Records."

"OK, Charlie. Coming up." Caruso was singing "Mother Macree."

As I listened to Enrico Caruso for the first time, I was really enchanted. I could remember Dad telling me what a fantastic voice he had, but I had no idea about the depth of his voice. I thought, "What a voice that man has, even though he smoked cigars. He was a better singer than Bing Crosby. My! My! And to think that Vina had a whole stack of his records. How in the world would any voice teacher teach you to sing like Caruso?"

I knew of only three other singers: Roy Rogers, Gene Autry and Dennis Day. Dennis sang on the Jack Benny

Show every week. He was a tenor. When Osa Lowry put a new nickelodeon in her restaurant, one of his songs was my favorite, Dennis Day singing "South of the Border." Some of the good old boys who hung around Osa's Cafe maintained that my favorite record was "high falutin' crap." I wondered what the boys would think of Mr. Caruso singing "Mother Macree."

The revival at the Methodist Church in Aldrich was filled to capacity. The choir was singing beautiful songs like, "Where You Lead Me, I Will Follow." A sea of waving fans occupied almost everyone else in the church because it was hot weather and there wasn't a breath of air stirring. I noticed the ladies who were fanning in close proximity to Carl and me were sporting fans that advertised a mortician in Bolivar. Upon further observation, I discovered that every fan I could see in the whole church was purple and white and, of course, contained the mortician's advertisement.

Carl remarked that with so many people fanning themselves, it looked rather funny. And it did. Carl and I did not have even one fan between us, but we continued to wonder where all the ladies acquired their fans. I told Carl that we were not advanced enough in age to qualify for a fan, and Carl laughed.

Carl and I had arrived early and found ourselves sitting in the middle pew, just a short distance from the altar. We had convinced one another we were going to be saved during this revival. We attached some comfort to the fact the revival was going to last a week. Since this was only the third night of the revival, we had plenty of time to make our decision.

We watched the church gathering expectantly, while listening to the choir sing. They were singing a song that was my mother's favorite, one she had requested to be sung at her funeral — "In the Garden." "I walk through the garden alone, while the dew is still on the roses." What a beautiful song.

At last, the minister came down the center aisle and approached the podium. He was an impressive young man, and he captivated Carl and me. In fact, as he stood at the podium, he seemed to be looking directly at us. Personally, I thought he was simply surveying the crowd. But Carl didn't think so.

When the minister began his sermon, he did not use highborn rhetoric, nor did he scream and shout (hellfire and damnation), a method of preaching that was familiar to both Carl and me over our young lifetime. But rather, using simple rhetoric in a modulated voice, he began the story of a young boy in a western town who had won a beautiful black stallion with a raffle ticket purchased hours earlier by his uncle. When it had been determined that the young man held the lucky ticket, a man walked to the lucky boy and handed him the reins of this beautiful stallion. The young man was ecstatic and asked his uncle if he could ride the stallion. His uncle issued a mild protest, reminding his nephew there was no saddle on the horse and that, furthermore, his nephew had never ridden a horse out on the open range before. The uncle's protest was soon overcome, and the nephew mounted the stallion. A small crowd, who had been watching the proceedings, cheered, and the local press took his picture as he put the horse into a trot. The horse soon began to run. He ran faster and faster and was soon out on the open prairie. The uncle was frantic to see his nephew, by now a speck, riding into the twilight, the horse on the dead run.

The minister stopped and gazed at his audience. "Here was a young man totally unprepared to ride the stallion. He had never ridden a horse before. He was traveling at breakneck speed and without adequate equipment for such a ride. In addition, he was riding through a country unfamiliar to him. And the worst thing of all, he did not have anyone to turn to for help. The horse was not likely to stop and let him off.

"How many of you this night are riding a runaway horse? You are frightened because you are ill-prepared for your experience. You don't know where you are going, and you don't know how to stop the horse. You want to get off, but you can't. People who do not know Jesus Christ are like this young man on the runaway horse. Your life seems pointless, without meaning, without relevance. A person who does not know the Lord is, like the young man, riding swiftly into the night. You don't know where you are going. You are lost. You have no one to turn to."

When the choir began to sing "Just As I Am," Carl and I approached the podium. The minister shook hands with both of us and said, "Carl and Charles, God bless you. Get down on your knees and pray that God may forgive you of your sins." We both knelt down at the altar. After what seemed like an interminable time, I arose from my prayers with tearful eyes, glanced at the audience and said, "I'm saved." The congregation laughed. I didn't think they should have.

Another dear friend of mine was Leonard Neil, the son of the town barber. Leonard and I trapped together one fall on Paul Toalson's bluff. I well remember the morning we had two skunks under one shelf rock that had two separate dens that went in under the rock. We managed to get one skunk out of the trap and kill him. The other skunk had drug the trap back into the den, and it was difficult to get out.

Finally, we were able to pull the skunk out to where we could see him, and that's when Uncle Dick (Leonard's nickname), while pulling the chain to extricate the skunk, received a full charge of skunk juice in his mouth. I immediately asked Uncle Dick if he could taste it. Writhing on the ground, Uncle Dick said, "It tastes just like it smells." Both of us had the strong smell of a skunk as we made our way into town. We were so thrilled because we knew that both of those skunks would bring, at the very least, $1. I remember that Uncle Dick kept spitting all the way to town.

When I walked in the house, I was immediately confronted by Granny, who kept squeezing her nose. After washing my face and hands, I started out the door for school.

"They won't let you in the schoolhouse, Charles," Granny offered.

"Yes, they will," I told Granny. But when I arrived at the schoolhouse, I was told by my teacher to go home. I hadn't counted on such a harsh decision. I knew my father would be furious when he found out that catching a couple of skunks had cost me a school day. As I made my exit from the classroom, my school chums mostly cheered.

When my father returned home the next day and was informed of my missing school, I found him to be rather upset. Dad really read me the riot act and informed that my days as a trapper would be over if I ever had to miss another day of school because of trapping skunks.

My tears didn't seem to benefit my position, even though I reminded my father that trapping was the only way I had to get some spending money. I told Dad I could sell some of the fish that I caught in the summertime and could sell a few berries in season, but trapping and hunting was my principal source of income.

Dad smiled and remarked that he knew I need to trap and hunt to make some spending money, but he wanted me to remember that school was more important than any other thing I was involved in.

"You need to get an education, Charlie. We are, at the moment, very poor. The only chance for you to be a success in life is to get an education."

"Don't you think I need to go to college, Dad?"

"Of course. You need to get all the education you can. We will see about college when the time comes."

As I think back now, I have to laugh. Uncle Dick the barber became a P.H.D. Professor at Loyola University. He served in this capacity for many years.

On a chance meeting, I asked Dr. Neil if he remembered the skunk incident. He laughed and replied that he was still trying to forget it.

One day while visiting with Clyde Perkins in his feed store in Aldrich, Clyde asked me if I knew a man by the name of Lester Pettigrew who lived in Bolivar.

"No, I've never heard of him, Clyde."

"Well, Charlie, before I was relieved of my job as depot agent in Bolivar. Lester came by one day to see me. I didn't know the man, nor had I ever met him. He seemed to know that I was losing my telegrapher's job, and his first remark as he entered my office was to offer his condolences.

"I proceeded to tell him I was going to put in a feed store, in Aldrich and that I would be all right. Lester looked pleased at my remark.

"'Clyde, I've got a truckload of cattle going to Kansas City. I've got to run.' He was smiling when he left my office.

"I did not offer an answer but sat in my office chair and took to wondering about Lester. He was, to say the least, rather nondescript, his dress being a dirty pair of Big Smith overalls and a gray work shirt. His brogan shoes showed evidence of dung found in a cattle yard, and his hat resembled one that had been discarded years ago. Also, I noted that he hadn't shaved for some period of time; neither had he frequented a barber shop.

"Lester did not give me the benefit of his company for several days, but during the interim I was given a full description of Mr. Pettigrew by two old-timers who seemed delighted for the opportunity to discuss the man.

"I learned that Lester was rich and he owned a considerable amount of land in and around Bolivar. After proper consideration, my two gentlemen informers agreed that Lester was a miser. They admitted that Lester didn't have much schooling, but as one of my informers said, 'You couldn't beat Lester out of a nickel unless you were a Philadelphia lawyer, and even then you would have trouble.'"

"Was Lester ever married?"

"Yes, Lester was married. But he had been divorced for a good many years. I heard that he mistreated his wife.

"I interposed a question to Mr. Lardiner, my favorite informer, hoping that I would not diminish his exuberance, nor his memory. 'Did Lester have any children?'

"'Yes, Clyde, he had one son who left Lester after he graduated from high school.'

"Where did he go, Mr. Lardiner?

"'I heard that he went to Los Angeles, but I'm not sure. Swede, the barber, told me a while back that the son was doing real good.'

"Didn't Lester get along with his son?

"'No, I guess Lester was a regular tyrant. I heard that Lester worked the boy awfully hard and didn't pay him much. Least ways, Adam left Lester, and he hasn't been back, to my knowledge.'

"Several days later Lester showed up in my office sporting a new pair of overalls, new brogan shoes and a shirt that defied description.

"'Clyde,' he said, with an air of exuberance, 'I'm gonna go see my son.'

"Where is your son, Lester?

"'My son is in Los Angeles, Clyde, and I'm going to fly out there. I've never been on an aero plane, but I'm going to ride one tomorrow. Bill Mosier is gonna drive me to Kansas City,' Lester continued, 'and I'm gonna give him $10 and buy his dinner. Do you know Bill Mosier, Clyde?'

"Can't say that I do, Lester. I know who he is, though.

"Lester, seemingly content with his announced visit, smiled and waved. I was busy with the afternoon train that had just pulled into the station. I would have liked to congratulate him on such a momentous occasion. Lester waved again as he pulled off the station platform in his ancient pickup truck.

"I pretty much forgot Lester after our parting with his announcement that he was going to see his son, until I met Bill Mosier in the Bolivar Cafe. I then mentioned that Lester had visited me at the Frisco Depot and he had told me he was going to visit his son in Los Angeles, and you were going to take him to the K.C. airport.

"Mr. Mosier laughed and remarked that Lester had decided not to fly but had taken the train. 'Clyde, I took Lester to the airport at his request. Upon finding the ticket counter for purchasing his ticket, Lester began announcing to everyone in earshot that he was going to see his son, and then he would explain to everyone who was close enough to listen that he lived in Bolivar, Missouri. This was a rather trying situation for the ticket man, who was attempting to either sell Lester a ticket to Los Angeles or get rid of him. Lester then began to ask people nearby if they had ever flown in an aero plane.

"'I have never flied anywhere,' Lester was saying, much to the amusement of the people waiting in line. The ticket agent was becoming extremely agitated and repeated his question. 'Do you want a ticket, sir?' At this juncture, Lester pulled out his dollar pocket watch and checked the time. Some of the people snickered.

"Ignoring the agent's demeanor, Lester asked what time the aero plane left and what time it would get to

LosAngeles. The ticket agent informed Lester that his plane would leave at 9:25 p.m. and would arrive in Los Angeles at 10:30 p.m. Lester just stood there looking at his pocket watch. 'Do you want a ticket, sir?'

"'No, by God, I don't want no ticket, but I would sure like to watch that damned aero plane take off.'

"Mr. Mosier and I had a good laugh, and Lester took the train."

I think it was the heat in 1936 that I especially remember. True, much of the decade from 1930 to 1940 was hot, with many areas suffering drought. But 1936 was a year that bears remembering. In that year, the temperature climbed to 100 degrees or higher for 21 straight days. During that time, it did not rain a single drop. Due to the interminable July heat, all of the windows and doors of the people's houses had to be open to keep from suffocating. The prevailing south wind that had always blessed the Village of Aldrich now seemed hesitant, or nonexistent. People who dared took their quilt to the yard to sleep. But they didn't get much sleep.

In Chicago, according to the Springfield news, hundreds of people were sleeping in the city parks. Several women had been raped because of this.

Food spoiled or soured in record time. A high percentage of the American people did not have access to refrigeration. Very few people had electric fans. The movie houses were very popular because they had air-conditioning.

If a person in Aldrich had the money, he could purchase ice at Roy Neil's produce house. When Granny sent me down to the produce for 5 cents of ice, I had to hurry home with the ice, which had been wrapped in paper. The ice used for our iced tea would be gone rather quickly because we did not have an ice box to put ice in. Grandmother would cover the small cube of ice with a clean tea towel so the ice would last through lunch, or as we called the noon day meal, dinner.

And also at this time, most people in Aldrich did not have running water. The need for bathing facilities increased as the days grew hotter. Most adults took their baths in a zinc washtub, accompanied by a kettle of hot water to help remove the dirt. Kids, like me, went to the Coffman Branch, or to the river with a cake of soap. The most popular place for summer bathing was on the Toalson Bluff and was called "the duckhole." The Coffman Branch had deposited a fairly large hole of water that comprised an area of roughly 30 feet square. This hole of water was anywhere from 4 to 5 foot deep with a bottom of fine gravel that made it comfortable for bare feet. And besides that, the duckhole had a sizable riffle that entered the pond from the east, even when scrubbing your naked body with Grandma's lye soap; that is, if no females were present. The residue from your bath, including ticks and chiggers and other contaminants, would flow downstream with the current, leaving the pool inexorably clean.

Getting back to Granny giving me money to get ice for our lunch. I can remember Granny explaining the ice situation when she was a girl 20 years old. That would have been in the year 1884.

"Yes, Charles," she explained. "The Sac River would begin to freeze over in November. By January some of the men in Aldrich would go down to the river with a team of horses and cut huge blocks of ice that were transported back to the block house in Aldrich. The block house contained an adequate supply of saw dust that was used to cover the ice blocks." I asked Granny about the block house, which had been gone for many years. Granny told me that the block house resembled a small one-room fort. But she said, "Yes, Charles, we had ice, even in those days. By the Fourth of July, there was ample ice for making homemade ice cream, and there was usually ice for lemonade up into August."

As the hot days and nights passed, I thought the story about ice and the block house were interesting. I wondered when the men of Aldrich quit harvesting ice. Dad told me they were still getting ice from the river when he was a boy. But Dad explained that the winters were no longer cold enough for adequate ice to form.

"Charlie," he said, "I used to take your mother skating on Sac River before we were married. Sac was still doing a good job of freezing over. I would help your mother get her skates on. We would build a big fire and enjoy weenies and marshmallows." Dad remarked that Sac would remain frozen over until the middle of March and sometimes later. But he said he thought the winters were no longer as cold. As I now remember our conversations, I wondered if Dad was painting a picture of global warming.

Almost all of the citizens in Aldrich were devoid of fans. My granny in Kansas City had a huge fan that she used on what she called "the sleeping porch." It sounded like a P-51 with the afterburners shot out. Not many people could pursue sleep with such a distraction. I don't recall ever seeing an electric fan in Aldrich, other than the large ceiling casablanca fans in Meyer's Drug Store. No,

I think Osa's Cafe sported one small fan. The fans that I did see came from morticians in Bolivar. I thought it was funny that the message on each fan was, "We Care." I can remember the little old ladies in the Methodist Church fanning vigorously. They were better than nothing. That is, the fans.

In such terribly hot weather, there was the eternal question of ironing clothes. Most of the clothing of that day was made of cotton, which had to be ironed. If you were lucky enough to have an electric iron, you were ahead of the game. But electric irons, like fans, were a scarce commodity. If you had to build a fire to do your ironing by using irons heated on your cook stove, you were doomed to considerable sweating. No matter which avenue you traveled, you were going to sweat. Most meals were prepared with either a cook stove or a coaloil stove. The heat coming from either one was not pleasant in 100-plus degrees. If you bathed in the morning and then ironed, you would need another bath. By the time you had cooked supper, you would need still another bath. The extreme heat and humidity made most people forego the rule of one bath per day. And on top of these shortcomings, you might not have enough water, for several people had their wells go dry.

There is one more irritant that your forbears suffered, and that was flies. Flies seem to prosper in the July heat, and they were everywhere.

Coy Stewart, J.C.'s father, invented some kind of concoction that he called TNT. I guess it worked, but I never cared for the smell. Of course, our family could not afford to spray for flies, so we just put up with them. Coy named the Aldrich town team after his invention.

Charles Dickerson

12 years old

Naval Air Force

Army Air Force

Army Air Force

Father—Ralph Dickerson

Nelson Dickerson

Audrey Dickerson

Grandparents—Robert and
Sara Dickerson

Eva Perkins

Grandmother—Eva Birt

Great Grandparents—John and Sara Perkins

Bert, Ralph and Willard Dickerson

Wife—Joan Dickerson

Marion Mitchell

Carl Benton Hensley

Dolan Crane

Part Three

Let me live in a house by the side of the road,
Where the race of men go by—
The men who are good and the men who are bad,
As good and as bad as I.
            —Sam Walter Foss

I still remember with great affection Ralph Taylor's Sunday School class at the Aldrich Methodist Church. Some of my buddies such as Carl Hensley, Marion Mitchell, Paul Vincent, and George Neil were, from time to time, in attendance.

One Sunday morning I remember that Ralph broached the subject of accountability. He started out by suggesting that children are not responsible for their actions until they reach the age of accountability.

Immediately, someone wanted to know at what age a person would be held accountable to God.

Mr. Taylor smiled and said, "That is a good question, Carl. For example, in most states you must be 18 years old to be tried for murder. So age is a factor in laws that govern murder."

Carl Hensley then wanted to know what penalty one would suffer if he committed murder before he was 18.

Ralph Taylor replied that a person committing murder before he was 18 would probably be sent to a reform school.

Carl addressed Ralph's last statement by remarking that he was only 16 years old but he understood murder was wrong. "I don't have to be 18 to know that murder is wrong."

Ralph replied, "No, Carl, you don't. But 18 is the age of accountability for murder, under the law, at least in most states."

"Do you think the Lord has a different view of accountability?" Carl asked.

Ralph Taylor smiled. I could see he was enjoying the interest shown by his class.

"As I said at the beginning, the age of accountability presents some complex questions. Carl, at what age do you think God should hold you accountable for murder?"

This question brought a response from almost everyone in the class. It seemed that everyone was talking at the same time.

As I watched all of the palaver, I remembered my conversations with Granny concerning accountability. She thought that no one was accountable to God for their actions before they were 12 to 14 years of age. When I asked her if it was the same for girls, she had replied that girls matured faster than boys, so their age of accountability could come sooner. But she never gave me an exact age, if there be such a thing.

"Many parents believe that human behavior is learned. In another vein, parents are responsible for teaching their children values. So, is it acceptable to assume that if behavior is learned, then values might also be learned, whether they be good values or bad ones?"

Ralph Taylor smiled and wanted to know if we had any questions. When he didn't get a response, he asked the following question: "Do you think values reflect behavior, or is it the opposite? Does behavior reflect values?"

Someone answered the question by stating that behavior reflected values. But I think that values can also reflect behavior.

"Then do you think that values and behavior have a certain coherence?" Ralph asked.

"I for one think that values and behavior are sorta related," I said. "For example, if you are a Christian, you will have Christian values. At the same time, if you are a Christian, you will display the behavior befitting a Christian."

"Charles, that seems to be a reasonable conclusion. Now, what about Christian ethics? Christian ethics would be compatible with Christian values and Christian behavior, would it not? Ethics generally would be the rules of conduct for a group culture. For example, in medical ethics the doctor is not supposed to tell everyone in town his diagnosis of a particular patient. In legal ethics, the lawyer is not supposed to divulge to anyone else what the man he represents told him.

"I will just mention situation ethics, which might have something to do with our discussion. Situation ethics is behavior, or values, based on a particular situation. For example, you find a billfold with $20 in it. You read the identification and find the rightful owner and return the billfold. That is one situation. You then find a billfold with $1,500 cash in the billfold. You seek the identification and become aware that the owner of the billfold lives in a distant city. If situation ethics are applied to this imaginary situation you could have the billfold contain any amount of money. Using situation ethics then, the question is, at what point or what amount of money would you disavow your Christian ethics and keep the money you have found?

"This has been a good class, fellows. I hope to see you all next Sunday. As we have discovered, the age of accountability presents some complex questions. We considered age, values, behavior and whether or not behavior was learned. We talked about Christian ethics and situation ethics. Maybe next Sunday we can wrap up this discussion if there is any discussion left. Bring your questions."

Ira O'Neil was Granny Dickerson's brother. He was a huge man, standing six feet, five inches tall, and probably weighed 230 pounds or more. Grandmother explained to me that I could call Ira uncle because he was my great uncle.

In 1939, Grandmother and I went to visit Uncle Ira at his home in Walnut Grove, Missouri. By this time, Uncle Ira was an old man, but he seemed to be rather spry for his age. He shook my hand and informed me he was glad that Sara and I could visit him and his wife. I, in turn, replied that I was happy to be able to visit him and I hoped he had some good stories to tell me. He laughed pleasantly, saying he would try to think up some good stories after we had dinner.

While we were having our dinner, I studied the benign countenance of Ira, wondering if he knew that

Granny Dickerson had told me about the O'Neil clan. Jasper O'Neil, Uncle Ira's father, was married twice and fathered twenty-three children. Jasper fought in the Civil War, in the artillery. Jasper, like his son, made an imposing figure in the picture that hung at the headboard of Grandmother's bed.

After dinner, I engaged Uncle Ira, remembering his promise to think up some stories.

"Uncle Ira, was your dad as big as you are?"

"No, Charles. I was a little bigger than my father. Now, Uncle Jack was about my size, and Uncle Jim was also a big man."

"Did you guys have lots of fights?"

"No, I had a few, but most men looked at my size, and I guess they decided I wouldn't be an easy person to fight. My brother, Jack, had several fights. Did Sissie tell you about the time Jack fought the minister of her church?"

"Yes, Uncle Ira, she told me that Uncle Jack had escorted his sister to church, a country church, and it was a very cold day. Grandmother said that uncle Jack was invited to come and take a seat with the rest of the congregation, but refused, stating he would stay in the back of the church by the stove. This apparently made the minister mad, and Grandmother said the minister was about as big as Uncle Jack. When the service was over, the minister stood at the door of the church shaking hands with the people as they left the church. Granny said when the minister shook hands with Uncle Jack, the minister swung a blow with his left hand and struck Uncle Jack. This resulted in a fight. But 'laws of mercy' it took half of the small congregation to separate the two men, Granny explained. And then, laughingly, Granny said that Jack's nose was broken when the minister first struck him. She finished by saying that is what made Jack mad. But alas, Jack did not see a doctor and let his nose heal crooked. The results of that fight left Jack with a nose that set to one side."

I asked Granny if Jack had won the fight, and she replied that he sure did.

Uncle Ira told me that he could remember Jack's fight with the minister.

"What year was the fight, Uncle Ira? Can you remember?"

"I don't know, Charles, but I would say around the year 1890. You see, Dad brought his family from Kentucky to Missouri in 1880. We made the trip in two wagons. Traveling in a wagon in those days was a lot of fun. There is nothing today that compares with it."

I had other questions I wanted to ask Uncle Ira, but one question took precedence.

"Uncle Ira, with the large family that you have, do you know where your other brothers and sisters are?"

"I know where some of them are, Charles, and some of them are dead. I have both brothers and sisters in California. The rest of my family is pretty much scattered throughout the United States."

I told Uncle Ira that I could just imagine how difficult it would be to keep up with such a large family. He agreed.

I mentioned from time to time that Grandmother and I had discussed different people in her family. I don't think Granny knew where half of her family lived or how many were still living. As far as I can remember, Granny received little correspondence from any of her relatives, nor did she talk about them, with one exception. She had a favorite sister she called Aunt Sissie. It seems that Aunt

Sissie had sent Granny a couple of letters over a period of time and then stopped communicating. Granny said several times she wished she could go to California and see Aunt Sissie. Such remarks always made me sad, although Granny didn't even have a picture of Aunt Sissie. I knew that Granny's $14 a month from Social Security would make it impossible for her to do any traveling.

After finishing an interesting story about the Plains Indians, Uncle Ira asked me if I knew where Jasper O'Neil, my great-grandfather, was buried. I told him I did not know, but I would ask Granny.

"Dad is buried in Greenfield, Missouri."

"When did he die, Uncle?"

"He died in 1917, the third year of World War I."

This information concerning Jasper O'Neil's grave would be remembered by myself and my wife. Many years later, we drove to Greenfield, Missouri, to seek his grave. The sextant told me where my great-grandfather was buried. Since it was Decoration Day, all veterans should have a small American flag on their grave. There was no flag on Jasper's grave, so I told several people sitting in a tent that were taking up a collection that I needed a flag for my great-grandfather's grave. The people were very nice to furnish me with a flag. We also put flowers on Jasper's grave, as well as that of Emma, his second wife, who is buried next to her husband.

When my new wife joined me in Chicago in the year 1948, I asked her if she remembered me telling her about my Great-uncle Jack, and she said she remembered.

"Joan, I want to go out to the Rob Neil residence here in Chicago and visit Rob and his wife, and especially, Uncle Jack. I think Uncle Jack has been staying with Rob this winter."

"What kin is Uncle Jack to Rob Neil?" Joan asked.

"Honey, he is Rob's uncle."

"And he is your great uncle, Charles?"

"That's right."

When we arrived at the Neil residence, Rob and his wife greeted us. "How is everything in Aldrich?" they wanted to know.

"Rob, Aldrich hasn't changed. I was there a couple of months ago. Nothing has changed. How long have you been gone from Aldrich, Rob?"

Rob laughed and said, "A long time."

Joan and I found Uncle Jack sitting in his room in a rocker. He was smoking a cigar, drinking a beer and listening to the Chicago Cubs baseball game.

Rob said, "Uncle Jack, do you know Charlie and Joan?" Rob continued. "Charles, Uncle Jack is 100 years old. Today is his birthday."

Joan and I wished him a happy birthday. I then introduced him to my wife, who almost immediately informed him that she could still see evidence of his fight with the preacher. Uncle Jack laughed and said, "Did Sissie tell you about my fight?"

"Uncle Jack, Sara, your sister, told me about your fight, and I told Joan. She thought it was funny." Everyone had a good laugh.

I asked Rob if Jack called my granny, Sara, sissy. Rob replied that Jack called all of his sisters Sissie.

Doc Kinder was a medical doctor in Aldrich at the turn of the century. My reason for happening onto this bit of information was my love of intriguing epitaphs, which I always enjoyed reading when I was in a cemetery.

On May 30, 1940, I went out to the Pleasant Ridge Cemetery to place flowers on the graves of my loved ones, especially my mother Audrey, who had died of spinal meningitis in 1930. At this time in history, we didn't have so many wars to consecrate. The Civil War dead had been honored on May 30 for many years, along with the veterans who had died in World War I. Armistice Day was the official day for commemorating World War I, and the date for this anniversary was Nov. 11. In the Aldrich High School, we always had five minutes of silence while gathered in the study hall to honor the war dead. I remember still a teacher reciting the poems "Flanders Field" and "I Have a Rendezvous with Death."

May 30, Decoration Day, was an important event to the people of Aldrich, for people from all over the United States flocked to the little country graveyard of Pleasant Ridge to pay homage to the dead and to participate in a bountiful dinner served by the various women's groups and churches of Aldrich. There was always plenty of fried chicken, mashed potatoes and gravy, salad and pie, and, of course, iced tea.

While ruminating on the sumptuous repast of yesteryears, I was staring at a very large black tombstone with considerable writing on the face of the stone. I stopped and read the following:

"Remember friends, as you pass by;
As you are now, so once was I.
As I am now, so you must be,
Prepare for death and follow me."

Below this beautiful soliloquy was another epitaph written in chalk that said, "To go your way brother I'll not be content, until I know which way you went." I truly loved the epitaph and vowed in my mind to remember it. I would ignore the clown who had written his epitaph in chalk.

When I returned from the graveyard that morning, I found Dad sitting in the front room reading a book.

"Dad, did you know a doctor by the name of Kinder?"

"Yes, Charlie. I knew him well. He was attending my father, your grandfather, in this house the very day he died of typhoid fever in 1921, the year you were born," Dad continued. "Your grandfather and Doc Kinder were good friends."

"When did Doc Kinder die, Dad? I forgot to look on his tombstone."

"He died in 1925, I think. I remember talking to him from time to time when I was the Frisco Station Agent about perceived shortages in the whiskey that he ordered by the barrel from a distillery in Kansas City. He always thought the barrels he received were short of full."

"Were they short, Dad?"

"Yes, Charlie. I'm afraid they were. It was against the law to have whiskey in your possession, unless you were a medical doctor. If you were a doctor, you could legally prescribe whiskey to your patients. From what I heard, Doc Kinder was pretty free with his whiskey prescriptions to his patients and his friends."

"Did Doc Kinder drink, Dad?"

"I don't know, Charlie, but I do know that every time he ordered a barrel of whiskey, after its arrival on the train, all of the railroad workers, the section gang and the track workers always seemed to know of the barrel's arrival. The minute the barrel was hauled to the freight room, somebody would be there to tap the barrel. The barrel tap was achieved by drilling a small hole somewhere along the top of the barrel. A small rubber hose was then used to siphon out the whiskey into bottles. After the boys had purloined a few drinks, they would put the plug back in place. Since the whiskey barrels were sealed, no one could tell how much whiskey remained in the barrel at any given time."

"Dad, I don't see why Doc Kinder couldn't find the hole in the barrel. Then he would know that someone was stealing whiskey from him."

Dad laughed. "Charlie, whoever tapped the barrels fitted a plug into the hole so perfectly that Doc probably wouldn't have found the hole."

"Dad, did you drink any of Doc Kinder's whiskey?"

"I didn't take any part in tapping the barrel, but I was given some of the whiskey by the boys who did the tapping."

Later in the afternoon, after my conversation with Dad, I realized that the repeal of the 18th Amendment had created illegal employment for my father as a bootlegger. Somewhere in the near future, or was it in the near past, I heard that Joe Kennedy and Franklin Roosevelt, two entrepreneurs, had brought an ocean liner from Ireland to the harbor in New York. The cargo was Scotch whiskey, etc. This ocean liner just happened to arrive in New York on the day the 18th Amendment was repealed. The ocean liner's full cargo of spirits reputedly gave the two enterprising gentlemen a quick profit of several millions dollars. I thought the analogy of the two gentlemen, as opposed to the feeble effort of Doc Kinder, was very comical. True, one mindset was ingenious, but for Doc Kinder to arrange possession of the only legal whiskey in Polk County was not to be sneezed at.

And then there was my father, who transported the whiskey he sold in a Model A Ford. His distillery was a large, illegal still in an abandoned coal mine in Frontenac, Kansas. His usual load, as I remember, was forty gallons, which required overload springs on the Ford Model A. Oh, my, how times have changed. And also amazing was the price of hard liquor at $4 per gallon.

∼≫

One winter afternoon, when in Stewart's General Store in Aldrich, J.C. Stewart hailed me and suggested the weather was perfect for a night hunt. I said I had nothing to do and would be glad to go.

When I met J.C. at his house about 7 o'clock, it was beginning to snow. We walked north 'til we came to the Coffman Branch. We then turned right into the woods. I thought it would be a good night for the dogs to work and remarked as much to J.C. as we struck north into the Mount Zion woods, where an old church was located.

Tip, my curr dog, suddenly barked treed off to our right. Tip had treed a possum, which I shot out of the tree. The other dog, Old Traveler, which J.C. had borrowed from Clyde Perkins, looked at the possum rather quizzically, as if he didn't know what it was.

"J.C., where did Clyde get that dog?"

"I don't know, Charlie. Clyde has sold him several times, but the buyers always send him back after trying him out."

Clyde Perkins ran the feed store in Aldrich and sold tree dogs on the side. Being terribly crippled, he had no way to check out dogs that he had acquired and asked

J.C. to see what was wrong with Spot. Clyde had always offered his dogs for sale on the basis the buyer could return a dog who couldn't measure up and have his money returned.

"Is that the reason they call Spot 'Old Traveler,' J.C.?"

"Yup, that's the reason. I think Spot has traveled all over the state of Oklahoma, Kansas and Missouri in his wooden cage. Apparently, he is not a tree dog, even at $20."

Our conversation was interrupted by Tip's bark. As we made our way in Tip's direction, I noted the snow was really beginning to come down.

"J.C., it's snowing harder now."

"Yes, Charlie, it is."

We found Tip sitting under a large oak tree continuing to bark. After examining the tree with my flashlight, I spotted the possum. J.C. held the light and shined it along my rifle barrel. At the crack of the rifle, the possum fell to the ground, where Tip wrestled it around a bit, while Old Traveler watched. I skinned the possum. J.C. suggested having a Snickers candy bar. I was hungry and glad for the treat.

J.C. laughed. "I don't think Old Traveler knows what we are doing or what a possum is."

I replied that I didn't think so, either.

Continuing north, J.C. and I followed a high ridge into the deep woods of Mount Zion. We treed several possum, but Old Traveler took no part in the hunt.

About midnight, we started working our way back toward the south. It was still snowing heavily. The night was very dark, with no moon. All of a sudden, we entered a clearing, and J.C.'s large flashlight beam was focused on a church house.

"Is this the Mount Zion Church, J.C.?"

"Yes, I think it is."

"It looks ghostly. Have you ever attended church there?"

"No, Charlie, I haven't. Have you?"

"No, I haven't. Do they have church here? Is the church still being used?"

"I don't know, Charlie. In the last couple of years, I've heard something about the church having two factions. I think Mount Zion is a Baptist Church."

Our conversation was taking place in front of the two doors of the church. I noticed there was a glass transom over both doors.

"J.C., hoist me up. I want to see the inside of the church." Putting one foot on the door handle or knob, J.C. helped me to stand up where I could see inside the church.

"Now, J.C., hand me your flashlight. It's so much stronger than mine." I shined the light down one side and then moved the light to the front of the church. My God, what I saw was ghastly. There was a man sitting in the front pew. He had dark clothes on and a black hat. He did not move when I put the light on him. I jumped to the ground rather hurriedly. "My God, J.C.," I whispered, "there is a man sitting in the front pew."

"Oh, Charlie, you're putting me on."

"No, J.C., you take a look," and I checked both doors again to be sure they were locked. When I hoisted J.C. to where he could look in the church, I handed him his flashlight. He immediately saw the figure. And he, too, came down rather quickly.

"Let's get out of here, Charlie."

J.C. didn't have to tell me but once. We took down a path to the road that led to the Coffman Branch. We were covering the area at a fast dog trot and looking back at the dark road behind us. We decided that no one was following us. All of a sudden what we think was a bobcat let out a terrible scream from somewhere close by us. J.C. and I took off like a scalded cat. J.C., who would attain the rank of Colonel in World War II, was leading the way. After running several hundred yards, we stopped to get our breath and almost immediately surveyed the road behind us with J.C.'s powerful flashlight. Seeing nothing, we resumed a pretty fast walk toward home. That night would never be forgotten by J.C. or myself.

During my seven-year stay with Granny Dickerson, I remember that most people didn't lock their doors. As I look back on those days, I can remember many people who did not even have a lock for their doors.

And it's amazing to me today to realize that most of the land in Polk County was not posted. There weren't many signs in the county that read "No Hunting" or "No Trespassing" or people who trespass on this land will be prosecuted. At the present time, the land is posted from one end of Polk County to the other. Signs that read "No Hunting" are numerous in the county, along with the "No trespassing" signs. Marion and I trapped and fished and hunted all over Polk County and were never told to get off the land. We literally had the run of the county, from the Sac River Bottom to the Coffman Branch to the duck hole on Toalson's Bluff and beyond.

"Dad, most of the people I see downtown have some sort of education. I don't know how much, but they don't have any money. They don't even have a car. The other day when the men wanted to play a croquet tournament on the new court, there wasn't anyone who could find a coin to flip to see who started first. There must have been ten or twelve men in that group. And these guys all have families. Poss Rotrock in the produce house had to give them a coin to flip so they could start the tournament."

"Charlie, we are in a terrible depression. That's the reason those men don't have coins to flip. There aren't any jobs in this country that I know about. And if I knew where I could find some employment, I wouldn't have the money or the transportation to get to the job. I think most of the loafers you see downtown are in about the same shape."

"Well, Dad, if there ain't no jobs in the country, what good is an education going to do me?"

"Charles, one of these days, this depression will end and people can go back to work. Every depression in the history of this country had ended in due course."

"Dad, I remember when you were breaking in a dispatcher's job in Springfield in 1931. Do you remember telling me about meeting the fine young man who was a graduate of Ohio State. You said he was a graduate mechanical engineer. Do you remember?"

"Yes, Charlie. I remember that he was washing dishes in the restaurant where I had breakfast. Every morning."

"Education didn't help him, Dad."

"No, it didn't, but he will be ahead of the game when the economy gets back on track."

One night after supper, my father and I made our way to the swing on Granny's front porch, with my suggestion that I would like to hear a story.

Dad smiled and, changing the subject, wanted to know how school was progressing.

"Dad, it's better now. Most of the people in my class are friendly."

"That's nice, Charlie. I'm glad to hear it. Now about that story."

Dad started by telling me he was called to Osceola, Missouri, to relieve the depot agent who was taking a two-week vacation. "I was on the extra board. I didn't have enough seniority to hold a regular job.

"The town of Osceola had several Native Americans living there, I found out later."

"Dad, do you mean Indians?"

"Yes."

"What were Indians doing in Osceola, Dad? I thought Indians were to be found mostly in the West."

"Charlie, I really don't know why Indian families had taken up residence in Osceola. From what I was told by some of the locals in Osceola, there were several families in the town. My story concerns one Choctaw Indian named Chief, the oldest Buck brother. According to some of the locals, the name Chief had been his name since he arrived in Osceola in the 1920s. He had come from Oklahoma, they said.

"I was anxious to get a glimpse of Chief, but I didn't lay eyes on him until I was almost ready to check out and leave. Then, finally, I saw Chief approach the square in Osceola, driving his bright red Dusenberg touring car. He didn't stop on the square, but I had at last been able to see him. He had on a tall cowboy Stetson with a prominent feather sticking out the top. He was smiling and waving at the locals and even honked his horn a couple of times.

"From time to time, I heard stories about the Buck brothers. I remember one local citizen telling me that young Buck had flown airplanes in World War I and he had a Jenny airplane parked out at his ranch. 'He likes his liquor,' the man continued. 'But so does Chief,' he said laughingly.

"My drayman, George Croft, who delivered the merchandise that came in on the train twice a day to the townspeople, told me several interesting things concerning the Buck brothers. I noticed that most of the stories were about Chief. His description of Chief was delightful.

"My drayman said Chief wore a tall Stetson hat with a feather in it, punctuated by a brightly colored Indian dress shirt with an elaborate neck scarf. 'He really dudes himself up,' the drayman continued. 'He wears buckskin pants, and he has as many rings on his fingers as he can fit on and fancy cowboy boots.

"'The other day,' the drayman continued, 'the two brothers made a bet right here on the town square. They bet $500 they could beat one another to the baseball game in Springfield. The brother would fly his Jenny, and Chief would drive his big Dusenberg touring car. Well, as it turned out, the brother made a forced landing north of Springfield, and Chief tried to make a square curve at high speed, ran out in a field and wrecked his car.'

"I remarked that a Dusenberg car must cost a lot of

money," Dad said.

"'Yes,' the drayman laughed. 'But Chief just ordered another new Dusenberg touring car, another bright red one.'

"George, that's the one I saw Chief driving Tuesday."

Dad said he asked the drayman where Chief got his money.

"'From what I hear, Chief and his brother came from the Cherokee Strip in Oklahoma. Their money comes from oil. I guess Chief and his brother have a huge income. Ralph, the other day Chief came through town in his Dusenberg rather fast, throwing dust and gravel on Osceola citizens who happened to be close by. It made the sheriff mad, so he gets in his police wagon and chases Chief. I don't think the sheriff could catch him in a months of Sunday, if Chief didn't want him to. But, anyway, Chief did inquire as to the fine.

"'The sheriff said, "You can't come through my town like that. The fine is $50." According to the sheriff, Chief grunted and presented him a $100 bill. The sheriff said he didn't have any change, so Chief told the sheriff to keep the $100, announcing he would be back through town pretty soon.

"'This made the sheriff rather irate. But as the sheriff thought about his run-in with Chief, he began to find the humor in the incident. When he got back to the town square and told the loafers about the incident, some of the boys said the sheriff got so tickled relating the incident that he laughed and laughed. In fact, he said everyone present had a good laugh.'"

"Dad," I questioned, "what is the Cherokee Strip?"

"Charlie, the Cherokee Strip was a reservation provided by the federal government to the Cherokee

Indians, who had been forced out of their lands in the East."

"Why did the government take their original land away? I mean the land they had in the eastern United States?"

"Charlie, the reasons are simple, but they are not good reasons. You understand from your study of history that the Whites wanted the land the Indians were occupying. The American nation was rapidly expanding West. You see, Charlie, the Indians, who were hunters and used to the open lands, refused to take the White Man's suggestion that they settle down and become farmers or live in one place, and follow the sedentary life.

"Charlie, there are five great Indian nations that settled in the Oklahoma Territory. There were the Choctaw, the Creek, The Chickashay, the Seminoles, and, of course, the Cherokee. The funny thing about this Indian migration to Oklahoma was that the land given to them by the federal government as a reservation was so poor that a common analysis of the soil in the reservation area, for the most part, would not even grow goober peas. And the funniest thing of all is that the land the federal government gave to the Indians for their reservation included a fantastic pool of oil that was to make many Indians millionaires. The federal government thought they would place the Indians on some land that was worthless, but they were wrong.

"The bad part of the arrangement that allowed the federal government to shuttle Indians from the East to the West was the depletion of the health of many thousands of Indians. Ever since the Indian Removal Act of 1830, the Indians had suffered the scourges of cholera, measles, small pox and various and sundry venereal diseases. In conjunction with the problems of their health, the Indians were plagued by traders, so-called, who plied the Indians with whiskey and set about to steal the Indians' land and money. And, Charlie, the land rush in Oklahoma in 1889 brought futher confusion and misery to the five great Indian nations."

One day when Granny went downtown to shop, I decided to look over the house. There were cupboards that looked interesting, and one large chiffonier, or chest of drawers, that had lots of interesting things visible when I looked in the first drawer. The first thing that caught my interest was a book titled, "The Sinking of the Titanic." Since I was only in my tenth year, I had never heard of the Titanic, so I kept it and decided I would read it. As I looked through the different drawers, I came across an old black pocketbook that snapped. When I looked inside the pocketbook, I found some pennies. I knew the pennies would buy a small sack of candy. I took the pennies and put the pocketbook back where I found it.

When Granny returned from downtown, she spied the book I had removed from her chest of drawers.

"Charles, have you been pilfering in my things?" I knew the book on the Titanic was ample evidence, so I said, "Yes, Granny, I was looking to see what was in the chest of drawers."

"Charles, you shouldn't bother other people's possessions. If you want to look at something I have, ask me."

"Yes, mam. I was sorta looking for my BB gun that

Dad hid," I said, telling a half truth.

"Honey, I don't know where your dad hid the BB gun, but it isn't in that chest of drawers."

"Granny, can I read that book?" and I pointed to the book lying on the kitchen table.

"Yes, Charles, you can read the book, but take care of it. Your grandfather bought that book for me before World War I started. I have kept it in that drawer ever since."

"What's the book about, Granny?"

"Charles, it's the story of a great ship that sunk in 1912."

"What caused it to sink, Granny?"

"It ran into an iceberg, Charles."

"Do you remember the Titanic sinking?"

"Yes, honey. I was in my late 40s when the ship sunk."

"How old are you, Granny?"

"I'm 76 years old, honey. I'm an old woman."

I spent the few pennies I found in my grandfather's old snap purse for candy. Granny was sorrowful for what I had done. "Those were the pennies in his purse when he died," she explained.

Although we were very poor during the Depression years, Granny, to my remembrance, never turned down a single tramp who asked for something to eat. I use the word "tramp" advisedly, but my terminology is correct for the era I am describing. I realize the word tramp would be a demeaning term in today's world. Some benefactors did refer to the man seeking a handout as a paddy, but all tramps were certainly not Irish.

There was a regular tramp path, so called, that was formed in an elliptical shape extending from where the railroad entered on the north to where the railroad departed Aldrich on the south. The tramp path was very obvious to anyone who came through Aldrich for the first time with panhandling in mind. As I recall, there must have been hundreds of tramps traversing the path during the '30s, or until the Frisco Railroad called it quits and removed the tracks. I think the end of what old timers called the "leaky roof," the railroad, occurred in 1934.

Least wise, the tramps would hit the path when the local freight arrived and try for a handout while the train was sitting in the station. This did not give them much time because the panhandlers were dependent on the train for transportation.

One widow who lived close to the path didn't give away much food because she requested that the man asking for food split some kindling for her cook stove. If the man agreed, he would probably miss the outgoing freight and would have to spend part of the day in Aldrich waiting for the next train. I guess the arrangement depended on how hungry the man was.

Some of the town's oldsters, when they saw the local freight come into town with people of every description riding on the train, remarked that the scene reminded them of a group of monkeys in the zoo. Every railroad car and every flat car would sometimes be alive with human beings.

Marion and I enjoyed watching the freight train bearing all kinds of people. Some would present a friendly demeanor, while others seemed sullen. When

Mitch asked a very friendly fellow if he wasn't afraid of being robbed while traveling with such a group, he explained that if he had paper money, he would roll it up smaller than the size of a pencil and put the money in his overalls in the compartment that was meant for a pencil. Mitch and I thought that was clever.

We never grew tired of conversing with the hobos riding the trains.

I remember that Granny hated alcohol, when she had openly told my grandfather before their marriage that "lips that touch whiskey will never touch mine." This threat apparently had kept my grandfather in line for the duration of their marriage.

When the 18th Amendment was repealed in 1933, there was a huge increase in alcoholic consumption in Aldrich. My dad, who would begin to sell whiskey a short time later, spoke out against the evils of strong drink to both myself and his mother.

Mitch and I answered the clarion call by putting a skull and crossbones on a piece of flat cardboard with a dire warning at the bottom of the cardboard that quoted the Biblical admonition, "Woe unto the man who puts the cup to his neighbor's lip." We placed this ominous warning on the screen door of the Meyer Drug Store after the store was closed for the night. The next day we checked early and found the card was gone. We did observe the drug store several times during the following week but found that Meyer Drug Store was not impressed by our threat. They had continued to sell whiskey to the local drinkers. So Mitch and I forgot the problem drinkers and turned our energy to other endeavors.

Shortly after this incident, Dad took me aside and told me he was going to start selling whiskey, that he was going to become a bootlegger. He said we needed money.

"Charles, I don't even have enough money to buy you school supplies or haircuts."

"Isn't it against the law, Dad?"

"Yes, Charlie."

"Dad, why do you call what you are going to do bootlegging?"

Dad laughed. "Because the old timers who sold whiskey carried their bottles in their boots."

"Will you make a lot of money, Dad?"

"No, but I will make enough to buy you some overalls and a Big Chief tablet for school and some of the other things you have been doing without. And I will be able to buy groceries and some milk. We never had enough milk."

True to his word, Dad did make some money and even gave me some candy and ice cream money. But I would rather have remained broke. To begin with, kids in the grade school would holler, "Your dad's a bootlegger." Soon, anyone who wanted a drink of whiskey, or a bottle, knew that my dad had whiskey to sell.

Later in the afternoon, Dad said he would tell me about my grandfather, Robert Dickerson, who had a problem with one German citizen who had arrived in the United States about six years before World War I. This gentleman, whom I shall call Fritz, which admittedly is a pseudonym, was a very successful farmer whose farm was about three miles from the village of Aldrich. Dad said the word around Aldrich got out that Fritz was constantly making disparaging remarks about the U.S. war effort and was praising each reported German victory. Dad said the men were really upset at what Fritz had been saying. Especially angry were the men who had sons in France.

One Friday afternoon, several disgruntled citizens of Aldrich appeared at the flour mill where Grandpa worked. One of the men asked Robert if he knew why they were there. Robert replied that he did. One of the town's merchants asked Grandpa what they were going to do with that Kraut Bastard.

"Hell, Robert, you have three sons in France, and I have two. I think we should pay Fritz a visit and shut him up." Most of the other citizens in attendance agreed. So 12 men, led by Grandpa, rode out to his house one night after dark and called him out.

"Dad, grandfather was playing the part of a vigilante, wasn't he? That's the way vigilantes acted out west."

"Yes, Charlie, but when the men gathered, your grandfather was asked about wearing masks on their faces. Your grandfather told the group that he would not wear a mask, that he wanted Fritz to know who he was."

So after calling Fritz out, Dad explained to Fritz what the men wanted with him, and what he had done to warrant such a visit. Then granddad told him they were going to whip him for his show of disloyalty to the United States. Fritz complained bitterly as the group tied him to a tree in his front yard. The man who did the whipping used a quirt, but Fritz did not show any pain.

When the man wielding the quirt stopped, someone untied the rope that held him to the tree.

Robert Dickerson addressed Fritz by making a short and simple statement. "Fritz," he said. "Don't make us come out here again." Fritz was silent as the men rode away.

Mildred Kirkpatrick was one of my favorite grade school teachers and a very pretty young woman. When she called me up to her desk one day and said she had a note she would like for me to take to my father immediately, I became wary since notes from teachers to parents were generally foreboding, to say the least.

Sensing I was uncomfortable, Mildred smiled and remarked that the note was one of friendship and had nothing to do with me.

I said I would deliver the note for her and ran out of the school because the school day was over. I was hoping to find Mitch or Carl and tell them about the note. When I could find neither Carl nor Mitch, I proudly produced the note for another unmentionable classmate of mine and let him read the note, which I also read. The note had, I decided, a sort of romantic flair.

When I delivered the note to my father, who sat in the front room reading a book, I was very careful to place myself at a point where I could observe my father as he read. Much to my surprise, he read the note without exhibiting the slightest concern. The expression on his face was blank.

By 9 o'clock that night, the contents of Miss Kirkpatrick's note to Father were spread throughout most of the 250 inhabitants of Aldrich. Later, Dad had several dates with Mildred, but nothing came of it.

In the 1930s, things were a little different than they were after World War II. I can remember the warning from the County Health Department concerning polio. Polio was the scourge of the nation in those years. The advent of polio vaccine and sulfa drugs were in the future. Tuberculosis was also pretty rampant in this decade.

I can remember my father pointing out a man who lived in the Aldrich community, but I can't remember his name. Dad said he would be dead in three months. He did die soon after our meeting in the post office from tuberculosis. He was a nice-looking young man with a family. I began to wonder at the mortality of humans.

Uncle Dee Dickerson, my father's uncle, took Dad squirrel hunting in the fall of 1916. As he and Dad crossed an old barbed wire fence out in the woods, Uncle Dee scratched his arm on the rusty barbed wire. A week later, he was dead. There was no such thing as antibiotics in those days.

There wasn't any penicillin, either. My mother had contracted meningitis in March 1930. She died that same month. Her doctor was to tell Dad years later that penicillin would have saved my mother.

People in the '30s, if they lived until they were in their 60s, usually sat out the rest of their lives in an armchair. Exercising was almost unheard of. I know my sweet grandmother always told me she had to rest in order for her arthritis to behave a little better. And, of course, the old people of Aldrich who read the Bible pointed out the verse in Timothy, which said bodily exercise is all right, but spiritual exercise is more important and is a tonic for all you do. (Fourth chapter and eighth verse.)

So, people in the '30s fought diseases like polio and tuberculosis, as well as meningitis. The great threat to life in the '30s was infection. The medical doctors of this era lost lots of patients to infection, and I couldn't go swimming, which made my life, at times, almost intolerable.

Jack Jones, I am using a pseudonym, even though I am not sure of his real moniker, was the subject of Dad's first story of the evening, while we occupied Granny's swing. According to Dad, Jack Jones liked to dance and liked his liquor, but the locals did not speak too highly of him, in part I think because of his dancing talent. Most people seemed to think Jack was the best dancer in the country, especially the women.

"Dad, did you know Mr. Jones?"

"Charlie, I was just a young lad, but I can remember his rubber-tired buggy. I never attended any dances in Aldrich because I was too young at that time. If Aldrich citizens wanted to dance, they would have to travel to Bolivar, Missouri. Even in Bolivar, the good church people frowned on dancing and described dancing, in many instances, as a tool of the Devil. I don't say that people in Missouri didn't dance, but I can't remember a single dance in the town of Aldrich through most of my teenage years, although I did hear people talk about dancing from time to time."

The news got around Aldrich that they were holding

big dances with live music up on the Bolivar Prairie. So Jack Jones, one Saturday night, cranked up his rubber-tired buggy and lit out for the dance, which, according to Dad, was about halfway to Bolivar. Jack found a large dance floor lighted with gas lamps and an ensemble of musicians. There were two men playing fiddles, joined by a young man on the banjo. There were two men playing guitars. The music was lively, and the women, who were aware of Mr. Jones' talent as a dancer, stood in line to dance with him.

"Dad, was this guy handsome?"

"Yes, he was, as I remember."

"Anyway," Dad continued, "Mr. Jones was really having a ball. After two or three dances, Mr. Jones would go to his buggy and take a drink. As the night wore on, Jones became less steady on his feet. Finally, about 2 o'clock in the morning, Mr. Jones decided to call it a day.

"But what Mr. Jones didn't know was that some of the people who knew him, or knew of him, had made a change in his buggy. They had put the small front wheels on the back and the large wheels on the front, thus tilting the buggy's front end up almost forty degrees.

"The perpetrators were watching Mr. Jones as he sorta stumbled through the dark toward his buggy. When he found his buggy, he made an attempt to enter the buggy but was confused. After some consideration, Mr. Jones walked around his buggy and tried to climb aboard. Again, he was confused. Finally, in desperation, he crawled through the open door, all the time hollering, 'Wow. Wow. You sunofa bitch,' to a skittish horse who was unused to the configuration of the buggy. The horse took off down the road with Mr. Jones sitting in the seat, but he could not see where he was going. The onlookers were delirious with laughter. And no one seemed to know how Mr. Jones traveled the six miles to Aldrich, but he did make it, probably because the horse knew where he was going."

Dad said he had it on some pretty good authority that Mr. Jones did not attend another dance on the Bolivar Prairie, adding that Mr. Jones was killed in World War I in France.

Part Four

No man is an island unto himself
Every man is a piece of the continent,
A part of the main.
—John Dunn

The first day of July in 1939 was steamy hot in Aldrich. I had just returned from a bus trip to Kansas City to visit my Grandmother Birt and brother, Nelson. As I walked down the big hill toward Mitch's I thought of the electric ice box in Granny Birt's kitchen that held the bottles of cold milk and the big circular fan that we slept under at night. I wondered if anyone in Aldrich enjoyed such luxuries. I certainly didn't know of anyone, unless it was the banker, Mr. Johnson.

Granny Dickerson didn't have a fan of any kind, except the hand-held fan she used to fan herself in church. Those fans, I remembered, were given out by the funeral home in Bolivar. I can still remember the name of the funeral home emblazoned on both sides of Granny's fan. One day in church, after watching Granny fan furiously, I jokingly asked her if she wanted the Pitts Funeral Home to bury her.

I said, "Granny, you are using their fan." She laughed. I sorta envied Granny and her fan because it was really hot in the Methodist Church in the summertime, and I didn't have a fan.

Osa's Cafe, the only restaurant in Aldrich, had an electric refrigerator and a freezer for the ice cream. Ice cream cones were a nickel; double dips and chocolate malts were a dime. Need it be said that nickels were almost as scarce as rooster's teeth. My taste in candy bars was rather frivolous. I could eat anything that was sweet. All candy bars were 5 cents, and when I had a nickel, which was infrequent, I despaired at the several options presented to me. I chose a frozen Milky Way. Good Lord, they were great. I wish I had one right now. My reverie was broken when Mitch met me at his front door.

"Charlie, it's awfully hot for 9 o'clock in the morning."

"It's gonna be a scorcher today. You wanna go swimming?"

"No, I'm too lazy to walk to the river."

"The duckhole is not so very far. Let's go to the duckhole."

"Naw, mother wants me to clean out the chicken house, so I guess I'll have to do it. I've been promising to do it for a week."

"You gonna go to the duckhole?"

"I think I will, Mitch. It's so damn hot, and I don't have anything else to do."

"Are you and Carl gonna head for Texas, Charlie?"

"Yeah. I think we are going to leave on the fifth, or thereabouts. We want to catch the mail truck to Springfield. Then we'll head out from there."

"I wish I was going somewhere. Does Carl think his

relatives will have a job for you guys?"

"He thinks they will, Mitch. I certainly hope he's right."

"There ain't any jobs around here."

"What'll you do if you can't find a job?"

"Hell, I don't know. I guess we'll have to come back to Aldrich. Wouldn't that be a hell of a note? Dad said that in Aldrich, with a population of 250 people (that's what it says on the green marker at the edge of town), there isn't hardly a single male who has full-time employment. The going rate for mowing lawns is 10 cents an hour. My dad said he wouldn't work for 10 cents an hour. Hell, Mitch, Dad is a rate clerk, a telegrapher. He's dispatched trains, and he's an accountant, and he can't even find a job. A distant cousin of dad's is a graduate of Ohio State in mechanical engineering, and the last thing Dad heard from him he was washing dishes in Springfield, Missouri. So, the only chance we have to find a job is to get the hell out of Aldrich."

"I agree with you, Dick. I'd go with you if it wasn't for Mom and Anna Dean. There sure isn't any jobs around here. The high school diploma we just received isn't worth the paper it's written on."

"I know, I know."

"Well, I hope that you and Carl can find a good job in Texas. I'll be pulling for you guys. Dick, you be sure and drop me a line when you get down there."

"I will, Mitch. Think I'm going to the duckhole and cool off. See you tonight."

As I started up the big hill, I began to rethink my conversation with Mitch. I was sorry that he was tied to Aldrich. His dad had died when we were in grade school, so Mitch had become the head of the family.

When I arrived at the house, I would pump a new bucket of water. It was really getting hot. During the summer, I would sometimes complain about not having anything cold to drink. Granny would usually advise me to pump a fresh bucket of water from the well. I would often remark that it would be nice to have a cold Coke. Granny would usually counter by saying that Cokes are bad for your teeth. True, the water from Granny's well was good and cold, but it didn't stay cold long enough to keep our milk and butter. It was not unusual during the hot weather for the glass of milk Granny poured me to be blinky. What a horrible taste.

The duckhole was a good half mile from Granny's house, but Paul Toalson, the farmer who owned the land, had made a good road down the Toalson Bluff right to the water. As I walked toward my favorite swimming hole, I wondered if any of the girls ever frequented the duckhole. Dad was always talking about someone's comb getting red. I wasn't sure what Dad meant, but I certainly had an idea. Down on Sac River, where most of the kids from Aldrich did their swimming, I would sometimes see one of the girls displaying more of her body than I thought was necessary, but I had a warm feeling when I saw something like that. I remembered the advice given to me by Rob Neil, the barber, some time ago.

"Charlie," he had said, while cutting my hair, "as long as your mule is in the barn, don't try to get him to come out. But if your mule comes out of the barn, you can lope him." I was hearing all kinds of things concerning my warm feelings, but no one would give me the whole story.

One day, in front of Stewart's Store, I heard one of the more prominent Aldrich loafers giving a discourse on masturbation. As I listened to him, I thought that I already knew the main facts on this subject. My dad had told me, very plainly, that if you masturbated very much you would go crazy. When I disclosed to Marion Dad's warning, Marion laughed and remarked that his dad had never mentioned masturbation, but that he was sure his dad would have informed him of anything so dangerous, if he had thought it was necessary. I thought of what Mitch had said concerning his father, as I listened to the gentleman make his point, speaking most directly to a man who sat on his immediate left and who my father usually referred to as a dunce. In fact, the man who I will call a dunce, I shall not reveal his name, was listening aptly to the speaker.

The speaker said, "Boys, they tell me that if anyone masturbates very much, they will grow hair in the palm of their hand." The dunce laughed loud and long, as did his companions, who took him under immediate surveillance. His covert move to observe the palm of his hand brought a roar of laughter. I didn't fall for the speaker's premise because I knew my palm contained no hair.

My thoughts returned to the young man who I had described as a dunce and who was still laughing halfheartedly. Sometimes the Aldrich loafers would play tricks on the young man that I thought were cruel. One day, they asked him to preach a sermon for a dead Rhode Island rooster that had met its demise in Roy Neil's Produce House. The young man seemed to enjoy the prospect of a sermon and was interrupted from the beginning of his sermon by one of the Aldrichites reminding the young man that he had not yet passed his hat to take an offering. Everyone roared as the young man said, "Amen," and passed his hat. Then, looking with mock sorrow on the dead rooster that lay stiffly on a banana crate turned on its end, he began to preach. Everyone, almost, roared with laughter. This event was more humane than some of the things the young man was subjected to. My last account of him was a short article in the Polk County paper, announcing his death in the local insane asylum in Nevada.

I do not mean to imply that the citizens of Aldrich were a heartless group, although I would suspect that there were some gentlemen who would fit that category. Most of the people in Aldrich were nice, but mostly poor. People often went looking for ways to entertain themselves because entertainment was so scarce.

In the spring of 1938, Charlie Meyers, one of my classmates in high school, approached me in Osa's Cafe one afternoon and suggested I should go with him to the summer CMTC Camp in Fort Leavenworth, Kan. I had no idea what a CMTC Camp was, but Charlie was quick to tell me all about it.

"Dickie, this is a summer camp of eight weeks, and its purpose is to train infantry officers."

"Charlie, you mean you and I can go to the camp for eight weeks and become officers?"

"No, Dickie, you have to attend the camp for four summers. If they accept you at the end of the fourth year, you will be commissioned as a second lieutenant in the Army Reserves."

"Are you gonna go all four years?"

"No, but I'm going to go this year. What do you plan

to do with your summer? Stick around Aldrich? Hell, there's nothing in Aldrich," and he laughed.

Charles was always a picture of exuberance in everything he did. We would both be seniors in the fall, and I didn't have much to look forward to do in Aldrich. Aldrich was a pretty dead place in the summertime. Of course, there were no jobs of any kind, except maybe some farmer might need a hay-hand for a couple of days. What Charlie had proposed sounded like a good way to vacate Aldrich for the summer.

"Charlie, will the Army pay you anything for attending the camp? I'm broke."

"Dickie, they will pay you $40 for the eight weeks. That's $5 a week."

"When do they give you your pay?"

"I don't know, Dickie, when they pay you. I'm hoping they will spread the money over the eight weeks 'cause I'm broke, too."

"How are you gonna get there? We could ride a bus. We could catch a bus out of Fair Play. That would take us to Kansas City, and from there we could get a bus to Leavenworth, if we had a bus fare."

"Dickie, your dad has a car. Maybe he could take us to Leavenworth."

"Dad is gone a lot, working on the extra board. I think he would take us if he were here."

"Well, Dickie, are you going or not?"

"I'm gonna go, Charlie."

As I walked up the hill toward home, I thought of the fight that Charlie and I had when we were sophomores. Charlie was a very good boxer, and it didn't take me very long to discover his prowess. So, from the time of that fight, I had become his best friend.

When I met Charlie at Osa's Cafe the next morning, I told him that Dad had come home the night before and had agreed to take us to Leavenworth on Saturday morning.

Charlie was tickled with my announcement and wanted to know if my dad was pleased that we were going. I told him that Dad thought my going to summer camp in Leavenworth was a splendid idea and that I would have a chance to learn something.

"But, Charlie, Dad said that he had never heard of the CMTC, but that if it was being run by the Army, it should be OK."

Charlie began to tell me the rest of the information he had on the camp.

"Dickie, the officer that I talked to on the phone last night told me that we could participate in all kinds of sports. I asked him about boxing, and he assured me that they had boxing, baseball, basketball, picture shows and all kinds of activities. We will train for six hours everyday except Sunday."

"What kind of training was he talking about?"

"Oh, you know, Charlie, such things as drilling and calisthenics. We will learn to dismantle a machine gun, a rifle, and the Army 45-caliber pistol, and he told me the camp had regular Army cooks that really put out good chow."

When I went to bed, I found myself reviewing all the things Charlie had told me about the camp. As I went to sleep, I was wondering about missing my dad for eight weeks.

While Dad and I were eating breakfast, I heard a knock at the door. Charlie Meyers greeted us with a big smile. "Are you ready for eight weeks of military life,

Dickie?" I replied that I was as ready as I could get.

Our trip to Leavenworth, Kansas, was pleasant enough, but I was especially nervous at facing an environment that was foreign to my way of living. When I voiced some of my concerns to Dad, he told me that this summer could be a great learning experience for both myself and Charlie.

"Besides," Dad pointed out, "you won't have to hang around Aldrich during the summer months, and you'll make $40."

"There are a lot of people in Aldrich who won't make anything like $40." We had a good laugh and wondered when we would get paid. Dad remarked that he would give me $5 to last me until payday. Charlie Meyers, whose father was an unemployed pharmacist, probably didn't have any money to give his son.

When we arrived at Fort Leavenworth, we were told to report to the administration building.

"Can my dad go with us?" I inquired.

"Yes, sir, your dad can accompany you to your quarters, as well. When he comes to visit you, he will know where you live." We thanked the lieutenant.

At the administration building, we were given brochures that listed our schedule for meals and the building where we were to be fed. Our quarters consisted of a tent on C. Street. I told Charlie I had never heard of a chow hall before and wondered if he had.

"No, Dickie, I've never heard that term before."

When the lieutenant noted that our living quarters consisted of a tent on C. Street, he inquired about putting us both in the same tent.

"Do you guys get along together?"

I answered, "Yes, we do." The officer laughed.

"Are you guys from the same town?" We told him we both lived in Aldrich, Missouri. He then instructed us to report to the main tent at the head of C. Street.

I told Dad good-bye and told him I would miss him. He said, "I will miss you, too, Charlie, but the summer will pass quickly. Eight weeks isn't very long."

Charlie and I reported to the top tent on C. Street, as ordered, and introduced ourselves to the commandant, who in turn, told us his name was Rod Graves.

He then informed us that he was the cadet leader of A Company. He was friendly enough, but he proceeded to give us a list of things we couldn't do and the things we could do. We listened to every word he said and tried to absorb it. From his instructions, I gathered that we were not to leave the base, that we would serve our turn as kitchen police, and we would obey the orders of the cadet officers who wore the blue felt under their Army insignia.

Rod continued his instructive manner by giving an example. "If a senior officer requests that you come to his tent and shine his shoes, you are to obey." He finished by welcoming us to the Army. "Do you guys have any questions?"

We noticed, as we entered the tent, that our roommates had already been there. The two bunks on the right side of the tent were made up, and the two empty bunks contained a neat stack of sheets and blankets.

Our two roommates came in the tent while we were trying to put our bunks together. Noting our difficulty, one of them said he would help us and remarked that only a military bed would pass inspection.

"My name is Derick Thompson, and the big guy over there is William Bradford." We shook hands, and we introduced ourselves.

"Derick, you will have to call me Dickey, since both of us are Charles. My name is Charles Dickerson."

Derick laughed and said, "OK, Dickey."

I could tell from the beginning that Derick was outgoing, and William was rather withdrawn.

"Derick, what is the netting for?"

"Dickey, the netting is for your protection against mosquitoes. The river is just a short distance from this camp, and, boy, the mosquitoes are really big."

"How long have you been here, guys?" Charlie wanted to know.

"We came yesterday."

"How is the food?"

"It's pretty good. We had breakfast at the mess hall this morning. The Army served bacon and eggs and toast or biscuits."

"Do they have Army cooks here?" Charlie asked.

"Yeah, they have Army cooks. But most of the personnel here are cadets, just like we are. You can tell how long a guy has been here by the color he wears on his collar insignia. Blue means he is finishing his fourth year, white denotes three years and red for the second year."

"Graves told us we had to obey the senior officers, even down to coming to their tent and shining their shoes. Who are the senior officers?" Charlie wanted to know.

Derick said he thought the men who wore the white or blue were in the category of senior officers. He said he wasn't sure, though, but we will soon know.

Charlie looked at me and laughed. "Dickie, we are here for eight weeks. Did you hear what the boss said? We can't get off of this post for eight week."

"By the way," Charlie addressed one of our comrades, "when do we get paid?"

William, a rather large lad, answered, "Beats the hell out of me."

On Monday morning, Charlie and I were notified that we would assume the position of so-called kitchen police on Wednesday next. Each Monday morning, we were to arise and be dressed by 6 a.m. After some senior officer called the roll, we were marched to breakfast. Shortly after breakfast, we were marched to the drill field and introduced to the complexities of close order drill. We were to march in a straight line, keeping the cadet in front of us square with our body. Charlie and I were doing OK with the drilling, but when we stopped for the second time to master the art of left face, right face, we were a little awkward. Then, when the drill master introduced the about-face, we almost fell down, finding this sort of maneuver comical. The cadet drill master did not appreciate the humor when he noticed our futile effort to do a 180.

On Tuesday morning, we each received a World War I rifle to compliment our close order drill. The concept of close order drill had now become more dangerous, especially when our platoon began to do the "to the rear march" bit. And then, "to the rear march, to the rear march." When this order is given, the platoon was to do two rapid 180s using the general mechanics of "about face."

Every cadet had been instructed to carry his rifle on his right shoulder, pointing the barrel at a 45-degree level, or angle. If you positioned the gun thusly, you would not endanger the man behind you by sticking the gun in his face. The only problem with positioning the gun occurred when the cadet got tired of carrying the heavy rifle and dropped the gun from its regular 45-degree position. The lower the gun became, the more the person drilling directly behind you had to dodge your gun barrel.

One day, after returning from drilling on a very hot day, a cadet approached me, wanting to know if I knew Charlie Meyers. I replied that I did, adding that he was in my tent.

"Well, you tell him for me that if he doesn't stop poking his rifle in my face, I'm gonna whip his ass."

I thought the cadet was serious enough, so I said, "You tell him, doc." That ended the conversation.

On Wednesday morning, Charlie and I were up before the birds to do our stint as kitchen police. I peeled potatoes and washed dishes, and we finished breakfast in good shape.

The kitchen police ate early so we would be ready to serve the main lunch to the cadre. When we sat down to partake of the early lunch, one of the cadets started telling the occupants at our table about his experiences as a golden glove boxer. He went on in some detail telling about individual fights he had won.

I looked at Charlie and could tell he was bothered by the hint of bravado being displayed by the young boxer. All of a sudden, Charlie addressed the young man.

"Damn, you must be tough." There was a silence that was deafening. The young man looked over at Charlie, probably not believing what he had heard.

"No, I'm not tough, but I can whip your ass any day in the week."

Charlie, standing up, replied, "Let's go see if you can."

An Army cook shouted, "No fighting in here. Go

outside."

Another regular Army cook said, "Come on, boys, we're gonna have a fight." Everyone moved toward the side door. Charlie's protagonist, being closest to the door, went out first, with Charlie following close behind. When both boys cleared the door, the young man turned to face Charlie, but he was a little late. Charlie struck him with a hard right, and down he went. The fight was over. Someone said the blow struck by Charlie sounded like a mule kicking a barn door. Leastways, Charlie's reputation as a pugilist was well-known, and his fame spread as he was winning acclaim in the ring, as well.

Dad had been right in his assertion that eight weeks would go rapidly. Charlie and I played some baseball and did lots of close order drill. When we weren't drilling, we were being instructed in the weapons of war and how to take them apart and put them back to together. The chow continued to be good, and we had all of the cold milk we wanted with our meals, which was a distinct luxury. We attended several movies, and all in all we enjoyed the summer. We finally got paid with crisp, brand new money. We did not partake of any crap games or any poket, but we did have a few beers at 5 cents a glass.

So, in the fall of 1938, Charlie and I returned to Aldrich High School to take our senior year. There was never any conversation between Charlie and me concerning a next-year return to the CMTC Camp. World War II was just around the corner. Charlie would end up in the Marines, and I would fly 35 missions in the 15th Air Force in Italy.

In the spring of 1939, during my senior year in high school, I can remember students gathering around the large Atwater Kent radio in the study hall to listen to Adolph Hitler's fiery speeches. The commentators of that time talked endlessly of Hitler and the threats he was making against other countries in Europe.

Our American history teacher called Hitler's tactics saber-rattling. He reminded us that Hitler had marched his troops into the demilitarized area of the Rhine River, bordering France, which had originally been meant by the French to create a buffer zone between France and the state of Germany. Our teacher went on to explain that the Sudetenland of Czechoslovakia, occupied chiefly by German-speaking people, at least according to Adolph Hitler, was annexed to Germany within the last year. Czechoslovakia would be the only country after World War II to emerge as a democracy. Austria also was acquired by the Germans in 1938 by means of an anschluss. Again, Hitler said most Austrians were Nordic and belonged to the Third Reich.

I'm sure that much of this European history, as presented by our instructor, was not taken too seriously by the students. But we listened and learned as we could without ever realizing Hitler was going to change our lives. In fact, Hitler would change the world.

One morning, after listening to one of Hitler's speeches, our American history instructor was asked to explain Hitler's speech.

He answered the question of the class by asserting that Hitler was not threatening Poland, and he mentioned the Polish Corridor that led to the free city of Danzig on the Baltic Sea. Our teacher could not foresee that World War II was only a few weeks away. But he explained, as best he could, the events that would lead to Hitler's invasion of Poland Sept. 1, 1939.

While engaged in the study of Germany and Adolph Hitler, I was asked if I had ever read Hitler's book "Mein Kampf," which in English meant "My Struggle." I replied I had never heard of the book. A cursory check of the high school library showed no such book. The next evening, a gentleman advised me that "Mein Kampf" was a roadmap for what Hitler intended to do. Years later, after reading "Mein Kampf," I discovered Hitler's plan for the Jewish element in Germany, as well as Poland and other countries in Europe. I learned that Hitler was imprisoned when he wrote his book, which was written in 1920, a year before I was born.

It was at this time in life I decided to pursue history and literature in college. That is, if I ever *did* attend college.

Marion, Carl and I graduated from Aldrich High School in May 1939, along with about 14 other classmates. Jack Burris delivered the baccalaureate address. I am sure the kids who were in our graduation class never forgot what Jack Burris said, even after the lights went out. Everyone in attendance at the ceremony was amazed that Rev. Burris was able to complete his address from memory, without the benefit of lights.

I remember well Jack Burris's words. He had started out by giving a welcome and a congratulatory message to the 16 graduating seniors and then followed by remarking that today's world did not present a very bright picture for today's graduates. He pointed out that the United States was riveted by the worst Depression in the history of our Republic. There were 15 million people looking for work out of a population of 150 million. And besides that, the world seemed to be moving rapidly toward a World War. "If there is a war, and the United States participates, many of you young men will be asked to serve your country." He concluded by saying he was sorry we had to graduate into such a chaotic world. "I wish you God speed, and may God bless each and every one of you."

The lights came on, and Mitch looked at me and grinned. "We have one more hurdle to get over before we test the real world."

I replied that it wouldn't be long because our graduation from Aldrich High School was Wednesday next.

Mitch bought me a package of Camel cigarettes for my graduation the night we graduated. I had already bought Mitch Camel cigarettes. We had a good laugh and a smoke over a Coke in Osa's Restaurant.

My Grandmother Birt had bought me a new brown suit to wear on graduation night, so I did not suffer for anything to wear. It is comical to remember Carl Hensley coming by my house on the way to graduation. My new suit, with the belted back, was to be complimented by the only tie I could find. It was, to say the least, a beast of a tie. Carl had a tie on when he came to my room. I told him his tie might look better on me than the one I have, suggesting that my tie might look OK with his suit. After some deliberation, Carl said that both ties should have been in a rag bag long ago. I agreed and put on the tie I had started with. I gave Carl his tie back. Carl suggested the ties were so bad it didn't matter who wore which tie. We laughed. Carl asked me why my grandmother didn't buy me a tie to go with my new suit. I replied that she probably thought I had some ties.

Years later, Carl, who had become a millionaire in real estate, called me while I was in Los Angeles and said he would come by for me and take me to lunch. I was not aware of his huge success but did think his new Lincoln Town Car was something. On the way to our restaurant, we reminisced about the old days. Carl asked me if I remembered the night we were trying to decide which of the two ties we would wear — mine or yours. I said, "Yes, I remembered."

Carl pointed to his tie and said the tie probably cost $20 or so. "But, Dickie, I was happier then than I am now, when I helped my dad in the blacksmith shop, and you and I went fishing on the river, and the day I gave you a chew of homegrown tobacco and you almost passed out. And remember the day we fought the bumble bee nest across the alley from Dad's shop?"

Getting back to the night we graduated, Rev. Burris was prophetic. Germany invaded Poland on Sept. 1. World War II had begun.

Most of the young men in our senior class served in the Armed Forces of the United States, including myself and Marion. Carl Hensley was turned down by the Army because of a serious knee injury incurred while playing high school basketball. Max Hailey, a friend of mine who was two years ahead of me in high school, was a B-24 pilot. He was shot down in Italy and killed. George Neil achieved the rank of Lieutenant Commander. J.C. Stewart, another friend, was a Lieutenant Colonel, now deceased. I was flying missions in Italy when Max Hailey arrived from the States. I was going down to Cerrignola to see Max on a weekend when I received a letter from my Aunt Lora Young informing me that Max was missing in action.

During my years in Aldrich, I had several other dear friends besides Mitch. There was Carl Hensley, whom I've mentioned before, the center on our basketball team. He and I went hunting frequently at night with tree dogs to hunt for possums and skunks, or coon if we hunted close to the river.

We also scouted Sac River in May to look for the suckers shoaling. Dragging suckers on a shoal was really fun. We were never able to locate the red horse shoaling, but while we were looking for a red horse shoal, we would usually find the suckers, who many times used the fine gravel of a red horse shoal to start their spawning. Suckers were not big fish. The average sucker would weigh from a pound to a pound and a half. Red horse, on the other hand, would weigh from three pounds to twelve or thirteen pounds. But the shoals of suckers and red horse were usually found in swift water on the riffles in water that was two feet deep to maybe four feet deep. One had to be on his toes to spot a shoal that would only be used for two to three days. We used to look for a patch of very clean, bright gravel, or little balls of dirty water if the suckers were just coming on. Then, of course, the waves and swirls in a riffle were telltale signs of spawning.

We didn't spend all of our time fishing. Carl's dad was the village blacksmith. I used to go down to Carl's just to watch his father heat different metals to a bright red and then form the metal into a useful object. I should mention that Carl's father grew his own tobacco.

I made the mistake of taking a chew of his homegrown

tobacco, and I almost transpired. I was deathly sick for several hours. That was the last chew of tobacco I would ever take. Even the thought of chewing tobacco curdled my stomach. Carl had a good laugh viewing my condition, for which I was eternally ungrateful.

It might be of interest here to follow Carl's career before he and I parted. In July of 1939, Carl and I ran off, headed for Texas. We had $5 between us when we left.

By the time we hitchhiked as far as Oklahoma, we were exhausted. We had stood on the highway all day in a boiling sun. In the little town that we got to in Oklahoma, I can't remember the name, we spied an old fruit stand that hadn't been used for years. We noted the platform running around the building and decided we would sleep there until morning. We had already been indoctrinated on the existence of rattlesnakes in the area, so the loading platform looked safe. We immediately fell asleep. About 11 o'clock that night, I was suddenly awakened with a stout kick in the ribs. I glanced up at the person doing the kicking and saw two things: A bright silver badge and a flashlight. Then I noticed the gun. A voice said in a sort of a guttural tone, "Don't move, boy, or I'll kill you."

I answered unequivocally, "I'm not going to move." By this time, Carl and I were sitting up. The sheriff moved his flashlight from me to Carl and back again.

"Where you boys from?"

We both blurted out "Aldrich," at the same.

The sheriff stopped waving his flashlight and just stood there as if he was studying us.

"Where you headed, boys?"

"Texas."

After what seemed an interminable time, he asked us

if we were hungry.

We said, "Yes."

"Come on and get in the patrol car, boys. I'll buy you boys something to eat."

We didn't tell him how tired we were but dutifully got in the patrol wagon and were transported to the dimly lit restaurant down the street.

The sheriff announced to the two or three people in the restaurant that he had found a couple of pretty nice kids sleeping out at the edge of town and wanted to buy us something to eat.

While Carl and I were wolfing down a hot beef sandwich, the sheriff addressed a man who had just entered the restaurant. "Jed, are you going down the highway tonight?" When Jed informed the sheriff in the affirmative, the sheriff said, "I've got a couple of nice guys here who are headed for Texas. You wouldn't mind them going down as far you are going? I don't want to arrest these boys for vagrancy." Jed replied that it would be OK for us to ride with him but warned he was only going as far as Centerville. The sheriff replied, "That will put them on their way. That's OK. That's OK."

Jed was hauling hogs to Centerville. Carl and I rode in the back with the hogs. Jed let us off on Highway 66 before daylight. As soon as Jed's truck was out of sight, Carl and I went out in a field that bordered the highway and went to sleep. We did finally make it to Texas but did not find any employment.

The sermon that had been preached on baccalaureate Sunday when we graduated from high school was coming back to haunt us. I remembered the words of the minister as he said he felt sorry for today's students coming out of high school because there weren't any jobs. Besides the lack of jobs, the United States was on the brink of war. He finished by saying the world we were entering did not present a pretty picture, and he apologized for seeming to be so pessimistic.

My father, after my mother's death, remarried in 1938. I did not get along very well with Dad's new wife. I was a little jealous of her, and I think she suffered from the same malady. My solution was simple, for those days. I would sign up for a hitch in the Civilian Conservation Corps. This organization had been instituted by the federal government, allegedly to take thousands of young men out of the workforce so that older men with families could have a better chance of finding jobs. The term of enlistment was for six months, and the pay was to be $30 a month for recruits and $40 a month for people in administration. Reserve Army officers were given command of the camps. All salary arrangements included room and board.

At the time of my decision to sign up for the CCC, I was working in the oil fields as a roughneck. My pay was, as I remember, $8 per day. The work was dirty, and I ruined most of my clothes. Also, I might add, working at the top of an oil rig was dangerous. The main drawback to my job as a roughneck was I only averaged about one day a week. Some weeks, I might get to work two days, but that situation was rare. I would have never sighned up for the CCC if I could have worked at least four days a week. The CCC became my last resort.

My father took me to the Lyons County Courthouse, where a group of about 16 young men were assembled.

Scuttlebutt amongst the group said we would go to South Dakota. Dad reminded me that he was sorry I had to go to the CCC camp to find work. "I wish you could have stayed here with us, but I know there is nothing here for you," he said. "Maybe when you have served your six months we can figure something out. I'll miss you."

The county sheriff called us all together and informed us of our destination. The sheriff looked the group over as if he were puzzled.

"I need a leader to take this roster and take charge of you men on the way to South Dakota." After some time had passed and no one said anything, the sheriff put the roster in my hand and said that I would be in charge.

"What's your name, son?"

"Dickerson, Charles Dickerson."

"OK, Dickerson. You are in charge of this group. When you get to your destination, you will give this roster to the commanding officer. You may also report to the commanding officer any trouble you had with your group on the way. Do you understand?"

"Yes, sir."

"One last word. You men are to mind Mr. Dickerson. He is in charge. I wish you guys the best."

With that remark, I boarded the bus, waving at Dad as I did so.

It was soon apparent that two of the fellows were troublemakers. I could tell they would cause trouble if given half an opportunity. I ignored them whenever possible, disregarding their snide remarks. The other guys in the group seemed to be nice fellows. The trip to Omaha was made without incident. Our quarters for the night was an old warehouse. There was a sufficient number of cots for our group.

The gentleman who met our bus informed the group
the same bus would pick us up and take us to our camp
outside of Wall, South Dakota. Giving us meal money,
the gentleman said we could go out and see the town,
but be sure to be back in the morning to catch our bus.
I was taking an afternoon nap on one of the cots close
to the warehouse entrance when I was awakened by a
shrill scream. I jumped up and asked what the scream
was. One of the guys said, "Dick, someone gave George
a hotfoot." I did not know who George was but learned
later that he was supposedly effeminate and his father
was a bird colonel in the American Army. George was
crying by the time I reached his cot. Now George would
stand about 6 feet, 1 inch, I thought, as I approached his
cot. He was holding his foot in the air. I noticed a blister
forming on the side of his big toe.

"What happened, Mister?" I asked.

"Someone gave me a hotfoot," he answered
sobbingly.

"Who gave you the hotfoot? Do you know?"

"No, I was sleeping when it happened."

The two bullies were standing close by, snickering at
everything George said.

A young man who would become my best friend in
days to come said, "Dickerson, one of those guys gave
George the hotfoot." The two hoodlums immediately
came to their own defense, maintaining that the
accuser was a damn liar, stating they didn't give anyone
a hotfoot. As this denial was heard by our entire group,
I approached the two hoodlums. Someone in the group
blurted out that the two people charged were lying.

"You two guys have bothered and picked on members
of this group ever since we left Kansas. I'm going to

report you guys to the commanding officer when we arrive at the camp." The tallest of the two troublemakers looked at me with a sneer.

"You are scaring me to death."

"I've had about all I can take from you two yokels," as I squared off with the bigger bully. There was no action because three guys, two of them much bigger than I, placed themselves right in front of the two antagonists. The big blond-headed boy (I did not know his name.) stated rather forcefully that he would kick the shit out of anyone who got on me. This ended the confrontation.

When we arrived at camp, I presented the roster to the commanding officer, along with a brief report on the bad behavior of the two hoods. As far as I know, nothing ever came of my report.

To say the least, this period of my life was sad. I was lower than a snake's belly in a wagon track. But the Gods were pulling for me because, after working one day on the work gang, I was asked to report to the C.O.

"Are you the gentleman who was put in charge of the group that came in from Kansas?"

"Yes, sir."

"What is your name?"

"Charlie Dickerson."

"Well, Charles, how would you like to work in the ranger's shack down in the Badlands National Monument?"

"I think I would like it very much. Sir, would my salary be the same?"

The lieutenant laughed. "No, Charlie. Your job will only pay $30 a month. Just think, you will be inside instead of out of doors with the work gang. It gets rather cold in South Dakota in the wintertime."

"Sir, what would be the nature of my job?"

"Charles, you would converse with the tourists, giving them directions. You would advise tourists on the history of the Badlands, etc."

"But I don't know much about the Badlands National Monument, sir."

"We will give you some brochures that will tell you everything you need to know."

After a most interesting conversation, I thanked the lieutenant and went to my quarters. In the barracks, I told Brad, when he came in from the work gang, about my good fortune. He congratulated me. Brad was the gentleman who stood up for me in Omaha.

My tenure as a ranger lasted several weeks and was a lot of fun. I would discuss some of the history of the Badlands with tourists who came by, covering the Battle of Wounded Knee, for example, the last battle of the Indians and whites in 1890. I would greet tourists while standing in what was called the Ranger's Shack. It was about the size of an Aldrich privy or perhaps a little larger. I met lots of interesting people.

One day two ladies came by and greeted me with a smile. One lady inquired about my job. Was I in the Army, etc.? I replied that I was in the CCC.

"Isn't your job a rather lonely one?" the other lady inquired.

"No, mam. I enjoy the solitude, especially when a few tourists stop. As you ladies can imagine, some days there are almost no tourists to talk to."

I viewed the elderly lady, who was driving, as a sort of Carrie Nations, when she asked me if I smoked.

I replied that I smoked cigarettes.

The two ladies, who were in a big black Cadillac,

laughed and drove off. I was rather shocked when the ladies who had proceeded up the hill to the lodge came back almost immediately, handing me two cartons of cigarettes, some candy bars and gum. They were laughing, and one lady, with the admonition that I shouldn't smoke, smiled at me as they drove off. As they left, I noticed the truck that always brought my lunch coming around the corner. I wondered what today's lunch would contain. The boys in the kitchen usually threw in a little extra.

After about 10 weeks as a ranger, I was presented with another serendipity. The company clerk, as I remember, had left to attend some sort of college.

After taking a typing test in the commandant's office, I was told that I was the new company clerk. I was advised that the ranger shack was going to be shut down until next spring.

I was now a member of the camp elite, and my new salary was $40 a month. And best of all, I had new sleeping quarters. Some memorable things occurred to me that I still remember. I can still see, through the brilliant sunny mornings, the great stone faces taking shape almost 50 miles away.

I really did think I had arrived. I was invited by the camp hierarchy to a party in Wall. During the night, I met a good-looking blonde about my age who was willing to climb into the back seat of the head cook's car. There was no one around, so we did some heavy petting that seemed to me an interminable time. After a period of time, I rejoined my friends in a bar, although I felt that walking was very difficult. One of my friends suggested I had the stone ache. I had never heard of it, so everyone in earshot laughed.

Despotism reared its ugly head in late November

1940. The commandant informed me that his nephew was going to come to the Wall Camp soon, and he would get the company clerk's job.

My answer to the C.O.'s announcement was that I would not finish my enlistment. His answer was that I had to stay for the term of my enlistment.

"I'm leaving, lieutenant."

The next morning, after saying my good-byes and fortifying myself with two large pork sandwiches, compliments of the cooks, I struck out for Wall, South Dakota. Wall was six miles, and it was cold and threatening snow. I was tickled to be picked up by a farmer in a Model T that looked as bad as I felt. But the farmer took me into Wall, where I could start hitchhiking on the main highway. I reached Granny Birt's house in Kansas City the day after Christmas 1940.

My erstwhile step mother, Lavernice Dickerson, taking my father's name for her second marriage (after the death of her husband), and Dad's third, was a sweetheart. During the 25-plus years I knew her as Dad's third wife, I was completely enthralled by this lovely lady. Her dimensions of intelligence were, to me, awesome, and her ability in all things historical were uncanny. Over the years, Joan and I were able to take Vernie, as I generally called her, and Dad on long trips in our motor home. Sometimes we would be gone for weeks. During this time we would spend innumerable hours around the campfire, immersed in antiquity, because Dad and Vernie both retained, with their excellent memories, fascinating tales of the past.

I can remember Vernie's description of her two grandfathers. One had fought for the North, and the other grandfather had fought for the South. The story was very interesting, in that both of her grandfathers were bird colonels. When the Civil War ended, both grandfathers came back to Missouri. Vernie said their farms were almost adjacent to one another, and as far as she knew the two grandfathers nor their families ever had any truck with one another. Her Yankee grandfather drew a nice pension until his death in 1890. The Rebel grandfather did not get a pension because the 14th Amendment to the Constitution states that "anyone who aided in insurrection or rebellion, that all such debts, obligations and claims shall be held illegal and void." Apparently, the hatred between the two families was ongoing.

And Vernie remarked, with a laugh, that anyone who put assets in Confederate war bonds usually wound up using the bonds as wallpaper.

I listened with rapt attention to Vernie's description of being in charge of a work crew at the North American Bomber Plant in Kansas City during World War II.

"Vernie, you guys were building B-25's...Billy Mitchell Bombers?"

"Yes, Charles."

"How many B-25's did you build?"

"We built quite a few, but my crew just worked on one section of the B-25, the hydraulic system, and sometimes the tail section."

"Vernie, how did you know about the hydraulic system of a B-25, or for that matter, the tail structure?"

"Well, Charles. I've always been interested in mechanics."

"Yeah, Vernie. But you were never around airplanes of any kinds before you took the job at North American."

"No, but I learned my job responsibilities pretty quickly, so I knew more about the B-25 than anyone on my crew."

My stepmother and I had many memorable conversations over the twenty-five years she was married to my father. Vernie once remarked she had read the Bible through countless times. We sometimes locked horns on Biblical issues that I couldn't agree with, but I usually lost the argument.

Vernie, being a lifelong member of the "Church of Christ," did seem to find it difficult to explain her church's position that no musical instruments are utilized. I referred her to the book of Psalms to reinforce my opinion that her church should allow music in their worship services, but she laughed and changed the subject.

One day when Vernie and I were discussing morals in general, she shocked me by remarking that some of the girls in her high school class were telling one another "that when you try black, you'll never turn back." True, the high school girls who were making such a remark were of the 1920 vintage, but I told Vernie that I thought the statement was naughty, and she agreed.

Sometimes our conversations turned to our families where I was able to glean information that I had not previously been privy to.

Vernie said, "Charles," with that glint in her eyes, "I was in love with your father before he was married, as was Audry, your mother. But your mother got him," and she gave that jolly laugh.

"Did you go to Mother's wedding, Vernie?"

"No, I didn't. They didn't get married in Aldrich. Ralph and your mother were married on March 10, 1920. By that time I was in Kansas City and had met the man I would marry."

Vernie continued on with family talk, exclaiming over her husband, who had sired three sons and a daughter. "He was a good man," she had said.

"When your husband died, did you ever think about marrying again?"

"Not until I was told by your grandmother that Ralph's second wife had died. I still held some regard for your father."

I well remember Grannie Birt, my mother's mother, telling me she had introduced Vernie to Ralph and they seemed to hit if off. I met Vernie soon after she and Dad were married. I had asked her what kind of a husband my father was turning out to be. Vernie's past history had already been related to me before I asked the question. She had laughed and remarked she and Dad had not seen eye-to-eye on a suggested trip to Paris.

"Lavernice, why do you want to go to Paris?"

"Charles, my son Ennis offered your dad and I his apartment in Paris. We could have had it for the summer, but your Dad wouldn't go because jet airplane engines hurt his ears." She concluded her remarks, stating rather wistfully that she would probably never get to Paris. Then, laughing, she said Ralph was a great husband.

Other people in the family told me several things about the Hayward family, which to say the least, were interesting. Two of Lavernice's sons were millionaires, while the third son was very successful. The daughter was an executive with Phillips Oil. Two of her sons were engineers.

When I commented on the scholarly qualities of her family, she just laughed.

"Charlie," she had said, "my father wasn't too dumb. In the 1920s, Hubert sold an invention for $20,000."

"It was a mechanical device, etc., etc." I could not understand the ramifications of Hubert's invention.

One day, when I told Vernie she looked nice in her new spring dress, she replied that she was the "Ugly Duckling" of the Hayward family that was comprised of four brothers and three sisters. I took exception to her statement.

"You are not ugly, Vernie."

"Charles, my youngest sister Cleo was a beautiful woman." She looked at me and smiled. "She was Jackie's mother. You dated Jackie before the war," she said knowingly.

"Yes, Vernie. I did. What happened to Cleo? Jackie had told me her mother was dead, but that's all she told me."

"Well, Charles, Cleo left Kansas City in the mid-'30s after graduation from Kansas University. She went to California and secured a position in some company. I can't remember the name of the company. When the family finally received her correspondence, she was ecstatic. She said she loved California. And she said she was dating Howard Hughes." Her mother, after reading Cleo's letter, said, "Who is Howard Hughes? Is he from around here?"

Hubert, her husband, laughed. "No, Mother. Howard Hughes is the guy that owns Trans World Airlines. He is a very rich man. He is also a movie star."

Her mother said, "I wouldn't think that Cleo would have anything to do with some high mucky mucky like that."

"Charles, the family received notification that Cleo was dead. She had committed suicide at age 40. When we went to California to pick up the body, no one seemed to know anything about Cleo's death. We brought her home. She is buried in Greenfield, Missouri. And the strangest thing happened. Someone put yellow roses on her grave for many years."

"Who do you think put the roses on her grave, Vernie?"

"We don't know. But finally, after several years, the flowers stopped."

When my wife and I went to visit Cleo's grave, I remembered that my great-grandfather Jasper O'Neil was also buried in the same graveyard. He had died in 1917. We visited Jasper's grave.

❧

When I was a young man, I lived in a state of perpetual wonderment concerning the Bible and religion in general. I attended Sunday School at the Methodist Church, where Ralph Taylor, my Sunday School teacher, explained away my questions without achieving any understanding on my part. I asked the Methodist minister the same questions and was given answers I deemed inadequate.

For example, I was told the soul was immortal. From this assertion, I could only assume a person would live forever in heaven, or you would be subject to everlasting torment in hell. This concept disturbed me. I did not disagree, but I did wonder. Was it true that all mortals would never die?

Then there was my question regarding the world's religions that did not accept Jesus Christ as their personal savior. If Jesus said, "I am the way, the truth and the life, no one cometh to the Father except by me," how could the Hindu expect to go to heaven, even if his religion was thousands of years older than Jesus Christ? And why did the Hindu call his heaven Nirvana? And there was Allah and the religion of Islam. A history teacher had told me there were people who worshipped Jesus Christ. Why would Jesus Christ allow the religion of Islam to overtake his Christian flock numerically?

I was invited into a Mormon's home for dinner one Friday night. This particular Mormon was a Ph.D., having taught mathematics for several years at Kansas State University. His home was a splendid structure, immaculate in every detail. The dinner his wife served was excellent. After we had finished our dinner, we retired to his den, where a fire was burning cheerfully in a large stone fireplace.

I looked at the good doctor, smiled, and inquired as to whether or not I could ask him a question concerning religion.

"Yes, Charles. Go ahead," he smiled.

"Doctor," I began, "you live in a beautiful home. The food you served at dinner was delectable. As I came in, I noticed you had three cars sitting in your driveway. You have certainly achieved the American dream. Yet, when we look out at the world, we can see the ignorance and the poverty of hundreds of millions of people who live in a state of perpetual starvation and degradation. They live without running water, medicine, doctors and all of the things we Americans take for granted. How do you explain this disparity between the Third World and the

United States? I guess what I'm really asking, sir, is how does the Mormon Church explain the grave differences between the 'haves' and the 'have nots.' Are these vast differences coincidental, or are they directed by Christ?"

"Charles, the United States has more people who revere Christ than any other nation on Earth. We are, in a manner of speaking, the stronghold of the Christian religion. It is for this reason our country has been blessed beyond human understanding. When you look at a map of the world, you can see that even our geographical position is superior to every other country on Earth. Yes, Charles, we have surely been blessed. That is the way we Mormons view the rest of the world."

"In other words, sir, you are saying, or perhaps suggesting, that the people living in the United States are God's chosen people, over and above the rest of the people on Earth."

"Not exactly, Charles. I *am* saying that the Christian nations of this world enjoy more of God's blessings. Do you not think so, Charles?"

"I don't think I could disagree with your last statement. At least it seems to be logical."

With this last remark, I thanked the doctor and his wife for an enjoyable evening. As I said goodnight at the hall entrance, I was handed a wrapped package.

The doctor said, "My son wanted you to have something to remember him by. He liked you very much."

I again thanked the doctor and bid him goodnight. As I approached my car on the driveway, I thought our conversation had been very interesting. I had wanted to find out the Mormon's position on the rapture and, perhaps, the subject concerning the Golden Plates of

Nephi. Perhaps another day.

The package contained the Mormon and Christian Bibles in bound leather.

⁂

In my sixty-fifth year, I returned to the small village of Columbus, New Mexico, accompanied by my wife and father. Needless to say, both of them were interested in stopping over in Columbus after I reminded Dad of our visit with the gent on the train, who had told us of Pancho's Raid in 1916, while Uncle Willard remained behind locked doors in the Southern Pacific Depot.

As we approached the main part of Columbus, we noticed several people congregated around an elderly gentleman who was talking into a large camera set on a tripod. The man behind the camera glared at us as we came within earshot of the proceedings. It seemed we might be disturbing his interview.

I turned my attention to the man being interviewed. He was a rather tall angular man with a mop of gray hair that protruded from a black Stetson.

We were pleasantly surprised when the subject in front of the camera turned away and smiled at us.

"Sir," I said, "do you mind telling me who you are and why this gentleman is interviewing you? You have an interesting face." I noticed the interviewer was scowling.

"Thank you for the nice compliment, sir. This gentleman is wanting to know something of my past life. I am the grand nephew of Kit Carson."

"I would like to shake your hand, Mr. Carson."

The gentleman smiled and offered his hand.

"My name is Charlie Dickerson. Were you here in

Columbus the night Pancho Villa made his raid?" I asked expectantly.

"Yes, son, I was. See that house on the left side of the street? I was living there with my mother when Pancho rode into town. But if you will look down this street on the right, you will see a stone house. That is where my mother and I holed up during the raid. Mr. and Mrs. Kirkland, who lived in the stone house, motioned for us to come over to their house soon after the raid started, suggesting their stone house might be a safer place to be.

"We had no more than entered the Kirkland residence when Mr. Kirkland informed my mother and me that he was going out in the street to see what was happening.

"Both my mother and Mrs. Kirkland pled with her husband not to go outside, where there was the sound of intermittent gunfire. Mr. Kirkland, with the rejoinder that he was sure the Mexicans wouldn't hurt anyone, passed through the door into the night.

"Within a matter of minutes, he was shot dead; and he had been so sure the Mexicans wouldn't hurt him. We could see his body lying just a few feet from his front door, but none of us would venture outside. His body lay where he was shot until the American Army showed up the next morning."

Mr. Carson also mentioned that Pancho Villa had burned the hotel, along with some other buildings, but escaped before the American Army got there.

The man who stood by his camera was growing impatient to finish his interview with Mr. Carson. We thanked him for taking some time with us and departed for the motor home, to go East.

When I was about 10 years old, I began to sense that my importance as a 10-year-old was secondary to that of the adults. True, my situation was slightly different from that of the orthodox family. My mother was dead, and I was living with my grandmother and my father. Granny had already raised four sons. And she was 72 years old when Dad and I came to Aldrich to live.

Several times in my youth I heard the suggestion that "children should be seen and not heard." I was, on several occasions, subjected to Solomon's Biblical admonition that "if you spare the rod, you will spoil the child." I thought I could see that most family considerations were tuned to adults and that considerations on my behalf were secondary. I did not feel especially unloved or mistreated, but I did feel compromised.

I must presume there are other fish to fry when it comes to explaining the foibles of adult behavior toward children in the decade of the 1930s. For example, if a child received a whipping at school, he usually received another one when he got home. Fortunately, the teacher was 99-percent right in deliberations concerning punishment.

With mannerly deference to the opponents of the Christian right and the so-called pundits concerning their positions on how to discipline children in our public schools, I would like to make a few observations. I have lived and experienced both sides of the issue in the matter of school discipline. I was a student in the perilous '30s and taught thirty years in the modern era. In thirty years of high school teaching, I removed one student from my class by force, and I taught hundreds of students in high schools from Alaska to Kansas.

My last twenty years of teaching was in a high school of 1,500 students. I was constantly bombarded with new terminology that divided everyday issues in the classroom. When we failed to discipline children, we said we were trying to help them achieve self-esteem. The new era brought pornography and profanity, and society said we were recognizing the First Amendment right of "freedom of expression."

So I traveled the road, starting with Clark Gable's famous utterance in the last scene of "Gone With the Wind," when he made his famous statement, "Frankly, my dear, I don't give a damn." A lady sitting in front of me in a theater in Lyons, Kansas, was visibly aghast at Mr. Gable's remark. She turned to the lady sitting next to her and said, "He said, 'damn.'" That incident occurred in 1940.

The question of values being taught in the public schools also became an on-going question. Whose values?

In retrospect, I cannot imagine my Sunday school teachers in the Christian Church, and later the Methodist Church, giving too much credence to moral pluralism or multiculturalism. True, these words never existed in those days, but the inferences were there, as well as the alternative lifestyles. However, we did not use that definition, but we knew what it meant. Maybe.

I realize that society was not very sophisticated in the 1930s. But we students did have a little help in determining values. We had a copy of the Ten Commandments posted in most of the classrooms.

My career in the Aldrich school system was replete

with various forms of punishment. Noble Neil, one of my grade school teachers, spanked Marion and me four times in one school day.

I can remember one comical incident that occurred when I was in the fifth grade. Miss Hartley, the teacher, called me up to her desk and swatted me several times with a paddle. I returned to my seat and bravely announced in a well-modulated voice to George Powell, my classmate sitting next to me, that it didn't hurt. Miss Hartley, noting my remark to George, who had laughed out loud as I took my seat, proceeded to my seat and demanded George tell her what I had said. George remained quiet.

"George, if you don't tell me what Charles said, I'll whip you."

George immediately succumbed to Miss Hartley's threat and said with a loud guffaw, "He said it didn't hurt."

Miss Hartley, now red-faced and very angry, directed me to come to her desk, exclaiming that this time she would make it hurt. True to her word, the second spanking really hurt. My eyes were filled with tears when I returned to my seat. Years later, Miss Hartley and I had a good laugh over the incident.

Several years after that, I met my English teacher at Pleasant Ridge, where my mother is buried. Our meeting occurred on the old-fashioned Decoration Day, May 30. I recognized Mrs. Wallace as she walked toward me, smiling.

"Charles, honey, it's good to see you. It's been a long time. Charles, they tell me you are a teacher. That's nice. I thought you would be in the penitentiary by now," and she laughed.

I introduced my wife to Mrs. Wallace, who then commented that I had a very pretty wife. I thanked her. As we walked off toward my brother's grave, Joan looked at me very quizzically and wanted to know why Mrs. Wallace had made such a remark.

"Joan, she is a classical humorist." I laughed pleasantly.

On Nov. 11 each year, there was a three-minute moment of silence commemorating the brave soldiers of World War I.

I walked to school in all kinds of weather, a quarter of a mile each way. Fortunately, I was never attacked by timber wolves. At this point in time, the "Christian right" did not exist, and Charles Baldwin's American Civil Liberties Union was in its infancy. This decade preceded the ban on prayer in public schools, and the high school was always open to any group use, no matter what affiliation they represented.

Now in a lesser sense, adults ate first at the main table, in case there was more than one table, or if my table manners were not acceptable to Dad, I would be asked to leave the table. Children slept on the floor, in the case of company, and there were not chairs for the children, unless and until all of the adults had been seated.

The children rode in the back of the wagon. Hickory switches and razor straps were in vogue. My father's favorite punishment, other than a whipping with leather strap, was to have me sit in a chair for an hour or so. If my sin transgressed the chair as punishment, I would be told to undress and go to bed. Going to bed in the middle of the afternoon was, to my thinking, cruel and unusual punishment under the Eighth Amendment to the federal Constitution. But Dad never seemed to understand my

Constitutional rights.

I should mention that school discipline was also pretty tough. You could not last long in the public schools in the 1930s if you didn't present decent behavior.

Please understand that I am not casting aspersions on the parents or the schools of the 1930s. I am merely trying to establish some minimal rapport between then and now.

I just recently noticed an article in one of the leading magazines, authored by a sociologist, that said we now have a cult of children worshippers in the United States. This makes children the king of the road. Parents have made the choice. If this be true, we have an inversion of values between the parents of today's children and the parents and children of yesteryears. I understand that much of what happened in the public schools of the 1930s could not be emulated today. That generation is gone with the wind.

Part Five

*We are at the point where we must decide
whether we are to honor the concept of a
plural society which gains strength through
diversity, or whether we are to have bitter
fragmentation that will result in perpetual
tension and strife.*
—*Earl Warren*

The following editorials represent my last will and testament as I perceive the world. I am not seeking accord for what I believe. My positions on these rather complex subjects surely do not find much favor with today's generations. But as I often said in a classroom at the end of the day, "Whether or not you agreed with the subject, I trust that you learned to think."

When I examine the modern liberals' position so prevalent in our colleges and universities, I cringe at their attempt to divert the path of human behavior from one of Christian ethics to one of moral relativism and political correctness. This philosophy makes no sense, nor does the Bill No. 281 in Congress, which describes so-called hate crimes.

The concept of school vouchers in an era of deterioration of our public schools is a must. Not only will school vouchers force the public schools to improve in many areas, but they will make it possible for untold students to get an improved education. I did my teaching in the public schools for thirty years and was grateful for the experience. Many of today's public schools are not doing an acceptable job. Teachers' unions across the country do not favor school vouchers.

There is a great shortage of knowledge in today's public school concerning America's past. Only recently I noted that many high-school seniors could not name the country from which we received our independence, nor could they tell in what century the Civil War occurred, nor could many of the group of seniors spell the most simple words. One literary pundit made the observation that "many young gentlemen today are looking for a six-pack and a sports car, without much regard for academics."

Students today are taught in the universities that there is no such thing as truth and no standard of right and wrong outside of individual choice. This thinking diminished the teachings of Christian ethics, which does not recognize the concept of moral-relevancy. For these reasons, almost no one can be found substantially guilty in a court of law, because there is an excuse for almost every crime under the sun.

University students today are subjected to professors who maintain all countries and cultures are equal.

The radical left has recently discovered what is wrong with America and has consistently displayed an anti-American attitude. They bandy about terms like "political correctness." The left took the anti-war position when we invaded Iraq, even though about 70 percent of the American people favored the war. At present, some of the left wing colleges and universities are refusing to allow

ROTC training on their campuses. In recent polls it was found that a majority of American males of military age said "no, thanks" to joining the Armed Services. They also indicate they would not favor overseas service in any future war.

I do not accept the Senate Democrats blocking the Supreme Court appointees by President Bush. Democrats in the Senate quote the U.S. Constitution, the President makes federal court appointments "with the advice and consent of the Senate." The Democrats are fearful of getting a conservative Supreme Court that will overturn Roe V. Wad, even though 56 percent of the American people do not favor abortion.

When today's federal judges note in the First Amendment that "Congress shall make no law respecting an establishment of religion, nor prohibit the free exercise thereof," I think the judges' semantics are skewed. When they demand the Ten Commandments be taken down within the confines of any government building or public school, they are not following the wishes of the Founding Fathers. They are most certainly prohibiting the Ten Commandments from being seen by the people who worship Jesus Christ.

They are most certainly prohibiting the free exercise of the Christian religion when they oppose the posting of the Ten Commandments, which are the center post of Christianity. The basis of law in the Western World is the Ten Commandments.

The Christian concepts found within the Ten Commandments are largely responsible for law in the Western World.

A little bird informed me that former President Bill Clinton favored making the World Court absolute over the U.S. Constitution. Thus, the U.S. Constitution would no longer be the Supreme Law of the Land. The ACLU wants to transfer U.S. sovereignty from our legal system to the United Nations. If this happened, the World Court could charge our generals in Iraq with murder for dropping cluster bombs on civilians, as an example.

Today, not one of the top fifty universities in the United States requires American history as a syllabus requirement for graduation. Even in our high schools that are beset by the same dogmas of political correctness and moral relativism, the difference between right and wrong has taken on a new character that borders on perfidy. A little bird told me the American flag stands for jingoism, vengeance and war.

The North American Man/Boy Love Association (NAMBLA) and the Militant Homosexual Colleagues are joining together to foster homosexuality. This movement comes under the concept of moral relativism. If you personally think homosexuality is right, then it is right. It doesn't matter that the Christian Bible says homosexuality is an abomination to God. If the people who profess this deviant behavior can get one of the fifty states to endorse the practice of homosexuality, then it could be legal in all states under the "full faith and credit" clause. I heard a senator say the only way around a state law legalizing homosexuality would be for the Congress to pass an amendment to the Constitution banning the law.

Separation of church and state, as a concept, made its first court appearance in 1947 in the case of Everson v. Board of Education. The term "separation of church and state is not found in the U.S. Constitution but is inferred in the First Amendment," says the High Court. The term itself came from the written works of Thomas Jefferson.

PBS radio is partly financed by the American taxpayer. Many people, including myself, feel the public broadcasts, whether on television or radio, fail to present a balanced program. The programs seem to veer to the left. Case in point, selection of art.

The American Civil Liberties Union opposes establishment of the English language as the official language of the United States. It also opposes the death penalty and favors letting convicted felons vote, an idea the Supreme Court will probably rule on in the near future. The ACLU has habitually taken a position on the left on most issues. For example, it opposes restraining illegal aliens from entering the United States, even though many of the incoming aliens will wind up on our welfare rolls and participate as Social Security recipients. The 8 million aliens who are now living in our country comprise a large block of voters on the left, who vote almost entirely for the Democratic Party. When you add to this number the Hispanic vote, plus the African American vote who consistently cast 90 percent of their votes for the Democratic Party, you can see why there are more Democrats than Republicans. Especially when you count the rest of the citizenry who give allegiance to the Democratic Party, you can envision a very liberal outcome.

There is not a lot of discipline displayed by the Congresses of the last forty years. Oldsters want more Medicare, prescription drugs and cost of living increases for their Social Security pensions. And they will vote for the party that promises them the most. Unions vote for the Democratic candidate because the Democratic Party has nominally favored legislation benefiting them. There seems to be a running battle between the "haves" and the "have nots," and the "have nots" are losing, according to what I read in the newspapers. I think it can be said that there are more "haves" in the United States within the Republican Party.

The Democratic Party does have its share of wealthy people, many of whom vote the conservative ticket. When I survey the makeup of the Democratic Party today, I can say with absolute certainty that I am not impressed with the overall intellectuality of the party. I apologize for my lack of political correctness. I do not subscribe to the concept anymore than I accept the proposed Democratic Party doctrine of total individual freedom. You can have so much freedom that you can succeed in losing everything, including your freedom.

The word "tort," under the law, covers civil wrongs for which an individual is entitled to compensation. Tort is of French derivation and means "twisted." Tort lawyers in today's world are fully aware of the twisting of the law, which is a process used daily in today's civil courts.

Liability insurance premiums paid by doctors to protect them from malpractice suits are going sky-high. Doubling and tripling of insurance premiums in one year is nothing new. Many insurance carriers have become insolvent and dropped out of the business because tort lawyers are getting huge settlements that many times run into the millions of dollars. Patients can sue their doctor in a civil court for such things as medical care costs, plus pain and suffering and punitive damages, if it applies.

The doctor's part in this drama is rather bleak. The doctor's services have, in most cases, a set price for each medical procedure, whether it be Medicaid, Medicare, or a private insurance company.

It is obvious the medical profession is not able to compensate for the rising cost of liability insurance unless they are willing to raise their prices. If doctors raised the price of their services, the number of people with little or no insurance would double, or perhaps, triple. The doctors seem to be between a "rock and a hard place," while the tort lawyers are laughing all the way to the bank.

The Republican Party wants to put a cap on the amount of money a doctor can be sued for. The Democrats oppose a cap. Wouldn't you know it?

The real loser in this situation will be John Q. Public because some doctors are taking the view "to hell with it," while many physicians are retiring early. Some other doctors are avoiding high-risk procedures, and obstetricians are limiting their practice or eliminating birth deliveries completely. It can also be noted that some doctors are leaving rural areas to practice elsewhere. It also seems quite possible to me that many talented young men will be attracted to some vocation other than medicine. We can live without tort lawyers, but it would be a little difficult without doctors.

Thomas Jefferson warned that "if a nation expects to be ignorant and free, in a state of civilization, it expects what was, and never will be."

***

America and the world have reached the greatest technological achievements in the history of mankind, but at the same time American morality is still in the Stone Age.

The Democratic candidates for president seem bent on creating laws that would furnish free health care and free prescription drugs to all Americans, including the rich and the very rich. American industry, of course in the main, favor this Democratic legislation. Just think what an improvement industry would see on their balance sheets if their expenditures for insuring their employees were suddenly taken over by the federal government, or the American taxpayer. As one could imagine, the cost would be staggering, to the American taxpayer, that is.

Liberals love feelings too much.

Republicans love facts too much.

To allow one or two malcontents, or thugs, in any public school, to raise hell and keep the other students from learning, is a crime against humanity. Liberal teachers would offer to reason with such students, maintaining that you couldn't kick the renegades out of school and would allow them back in the classroom.

Conservative teachers, in the same situation, would offer up a warning to misbehaved students, and if they didn't straighten up, they would suggest that the students be removed from their class.

The liberals would ask the same old question. Where would we put such students? The conservative teachers would reply, "Let society handle them because the well-being of two anti-students is not as important as the other 23 students in the typical class of 25. The liberal teachers generally win out, as you can see when you look at the nation's schools.

With mannerly deference to the opponents of the Christian right, and the pundits, concerning their positions on how to discipline children in our public schools, I would like to make a few observations.

I found the wisdom of Solomon in the book of Proverbs presented an interesting point of view on this controversial subject. His instruction on the disciplining of children, however, seems to be at odds with many modern parents of this age, as well as school officials, teachers and behavioral scientists.

Let's take a look at Solomon's prescription or rationale for this public school dilemma.

From the book of Proverbs in The Living Bible:

Proverbs 13:24 — If you refuse to discipline your son, it proves you don't love him; for if you love him you will be prompt to punish him.

Proverbs 19:18 — Discipline your son in his early years while there is hope. If you don't, you will ruin his life.

Proverbs 22:6 — Teach a child to choose the right path, and when he is older he will remain upon it.

Proverbs 22:15 — A youngster's heart is filled with rebellion, but punishment will drive it out of him.

Proverbs 23:13 — Don't fail to correct your children; discipline won't hurt them! They won't die if you use a stick on them! Punishment will keep them out of hell.

Proverbs 29:15 — Scolding and spanking a child helps him to learn. Left to himself, he brings shame to his mother.

Proverbs 29:17 — Discipline your son and he will give you happiness and peace of mind.

Proverbs 29:19 — Sometimes mere words are not enough – discipline is needed for the words may not be heeded.

From the ancient talmud comes a bit of advice on the rearing of children. "If you don't bend the twig of a vine when it is young, you cannot bend it when it hardens."

Then there is the biblical admonition that to spare the rod will spoil the child. And in Leviticus, the Lord warned the Jews not to eat fat: and in the book of Job, the people were counseled to wash their hands. These little tidbits of ancient wisdom, thousands of years old, sometimes call to question the wisdom of us moderns.

I have recently noted that the Iraqis declared the American Barbie doll to be one of the signs of American decadence. On same day, in the newspaper, I saw where the Taliban fighters in Afghanistan were stipulating that any Arab caught shaving off his mustache, or any female not wearing her full regalia of the sari and the veil, or anyone listening to Western music would have his or her nose cut off. The harshness of this proclamation causes me to wonder if decadence is the right word for the Iraqis' description of America. I suggest that Iraqis should define their own behavior as that of a heathen nation who has not, as yet, emerged from the Dark Ages.

When I see hundreds of Shiites practicing self flagellation on the TV screen, I think of tribal natives in Africa who have followed this insipid procedure for thousands of years, utterly devoid of modern civilization. These native Africans do not, however, castigate America for being decadent.

The U.S. Department of Defense is being sued by a group of law professors, law schools, and students who are alleging the university requirement that law schools allow military recruiters to come on campus violates the First Amendment. Several universities have, in the past, barred military recruiters because of the military's ban on homosexuals, which the litigants said violated nondiscrimination rules.

The U.S. Department of Defense also denies federal money to institutions of higher learning that will not allow the military to recruit or foster ROTC programs on their campuses due to antiwar sentiments. Many of America's universities have become extremely liberal in the last thirty years.

Some Democrat in Kansas City wishing to bolster the concept that the Republican programs are designed to help the rich and the rich do not pay enough income tax quoted John Kenneth Galbraith, who said, "The modern conservative is engaged in one of man's oldest exercises in moral philosophy. That is the search for a superior moral justification for selfishness."

The question of reparations being paid by the American government to the descendants of slaves is a childish request that has no merit. The fact that our government gave over a billion dollars to Japanese interns following the second World War was very controversial. The United States had incurred a very large debt fighting the war, plus the loss of American lives. Many people in the United States did not favor reparation payments to the Japanese. But it must be remembered that large numbers of Japanese, who were actually American citizens, lost homes, businesses, land and other personal property. The U.S. government was addressing both the loss of property and the loss of citizenship in determining the amount of reparations to be paid. The calculations for determining the amount of payments to the Japanese was readily available, while the means of calculating reparations payments for 2 million Negroes over 200 years ago was not.

The ELF, better known as the Earth Liberation Front, which has two basic causes — animal rights and saving the environment — has recently been charged with burning millions of dollars of mostly new construction. The reason for ELF turning to arson to perpetuate its philosophy was two-fold. The new buildings were going to destroy the environment, as well as sacrifice the animal habitat.

Not long ago, ELF torched a large automobile agency on the West Coast in order to destroy a number of new sports utility vehicles because SUVs are gas guzzlers that pollute the air.

There are many other examples of this non-sensical behavior, but one of my favorites is the demand by ELF that we find a more humane way to butcher chickens, hogs and other farm animals in our packing plants.

Thus, we have American citizen-terrorists who are demented in their departure from reality. It takes people whose nature most of us do not understand to follow the path of ELF.

In the Muslim country of Nigeria, a 29-year-old married woman with two children was sentenced to death by stoning for what the court charged — committing adultery.

Indonesia is planning to make a law that would ban unmarried couples from having sex or living together. The largest Muslim population in the world is also speculating on doing away with black magic, witchcraft and mysticism if they can. Couples found guilty of living together before marriage would face a sentence of two years in prison. Extramarital sex offenders would be criminals, and a man breaking his promise to a woman he had impregnated would be sentenced to five years in prison. Wouldn't you like to live in a Muslim country?

I read a recent article that portrayed the reality of war. I will not mention names, but the article related to a luncheon engagement that a newspaper editor of one of the largest newspapers in the United States had made with a Washington author of some renown. The editor, a woman, had just returned from a visit to the Vietnam Wall in Washington, D.C., where all 56,000 casualties are recorded. The lady seemed very distraught over her visit to the Wall and was expressing her feelings to her companion.

"All of those young American men killed," she had said sorrowfully. "I can't imagine the extent of the anguish that reached across the land, or the remorse for such a horrible war."

Her male companion nodded in agreement, stating that he, too, thought the Vietnam War was tragic in its consequences. Continuing, the gentleman asked the editor if she had ever visited the little Dunker Church just north of Sharpsburg, Virginia, which was a short drive from Washington, D.C.

"No," the lady had replied, "I have never been to Sharpsburg."

The gentleman then explained there was a monument there commemorating the Battle of Antietam during the Civil War, where 26,000 federal and Confederate troops were killed in one day. The lady editor was astonished and remarked in a rather subdued voice that she had never heard of Antietam.

The gentleman was, of course, perplexed by the lady's confession. He was wondering how the chief editor of one of America's largest newspapers and a graduate of a large Eastern university could be so ill-informed. Bemused by the turn of events, the gentleman went on to explain that America had suffered more than 5 million casualties in the four years of Civil War. The lady informed her lunch guest that she had enjoyed the conversation and hoped his next novel would be a success and departed.

At a later date, the dwarfs who are Democratic candidates for the presidency were screaming that the U.S. Army had lost 160-some odd men since Bush had flown into a Navy carrier and announced the end of the war.

Gosh, fellows. Peace and freedom have a price, or haven't you figured that out yet?

An English Jurist, commenting on the past history of law, was asked the question, "What is the law?" He replied that the law was beyond comprehension.

In today's malaise of modern law, the Supreme Court has said America's children have a constitutional right to view pornography on television, and the Supreme Court will decide this year if school children can use the term "under God" when saying the Pledge of Allegiance in school.

It has been reported on a major TV network that the ACLU is going to court to replace the term Christmas with a new version called "The Winter Holidays."

The ACLU is promoting secularism across America, as are many constituents in the Democratic Party.

Several analysts have charged the ACLU with being one of the most dangerous organizations in the United States. Seven hundred lawyers across the United States are forming an organization to combat the ACLU. The position of the ACLU seems to be a complete rejection of American principles. As Mr. Webster says when defining secularism, "secularists promote the view that public education, and other matters of civil policy, should be conducted without the introduction of religious element."

If anyone can find any logic in the aforementioned Constitutional analysis, please call me.

Printed in the United States
by Baker & Taylor Publisher Services